W9-CBA-847

Pitt Series in
POLICY AND INSTITUTIONAL STUDIES

MAKING COMMON SENSE OF

Japan

STEVEN R. REED

UNIVERSITY OF PITTSBURGH PRESS

Pittsburgh and London

Published by the University of Pittsburgh Press, Pittsburgh, Pa. 15260
Copyright © 1993, University of Pittsburgh Press
All rights reserved
Manufactured in the United States of America
Printed on acid-free paper
Third paperback printing, 1994

LIBRARY OF CONGRESS CATALOGING-IN-PUBLICATION DATA

Reed, Steven R., 1947–
    Making common sense of Japan / Steven R. Reed.
        p.   cm. — (Pitt series in policy and institutional studies)
    Includes bibliographical references and index.
    ISBN 0-8229-3757-3. — ISBN 0-8229-5510-5 (pbk.)
        1. Industrial relations—Japan.   2. Industry—Social aspects—
    Japan. 3. Manpower policy—Japan.   4. Industry and state—Japan.
    5. Japan—Social conditions—1945– I. Title.   II. Series.
    HD8726.5.R44   1993
    331'.0952—dc20   93-12871
                                                                            CIP

A CIP catalogue record for this book is available from the British Library.

Eurospan, London

Contents

Preface

The basic research upon which this book is based was not done in the field or on a computer but in the classroom. Over a dozen years I have taught courses on Japanese politics at the University of Alabama, Harvard University, the University of Washington, and Chiba University in Japan. Teaching is not simply a matter of presenting facts to the students. One must try to explain. Explaining often involves finding things in the students' own experiences, things they already understand, and relating those things to the new information about Japan. In other words, one must try to make Japan understandable in commonsense terms. Over the years I have developed a repertoire of stories that help make common sense of Japan. These stories form the core of this book. I have had to adjust them for the students of each of the universities at which I have taught. I hope I have adjusted and honed the stories sufficiently to make them useful to a broad audience.

I owe the greatest thanks to my students without whose efforts at understanding Japan this book would not have been possible. The Democracy Lunch group at the University of Alabama provided me with a forum to present the material and get feedback from an academic audience. I would also like to thank John C. Campbell for his detailed comments on earlier drafts of this book. Others who made significant comments that guided my work include T. J. Pempel, Margaret McKean, Matthew Shugart, and Annette Reed.

MAKING COMMON SENSE OF
Japan

CHAPTER ONE

A Unique Nation?

The Japanese do many things that violate American common sense. The most prominent examples are found in the economic sphere. Permanent employment — hiring workers for life — makes no sense to American management or to American labor. The cooperation between Japanese government and business confounds the basic American assumption — that business and government are natural enemies. Americans "know" that permanent employment cannot work and that government intervention in the economy necessarily produces negative results. We know this with certainty from our own lives, not just because some professor taught it to us in our college days. Yet Japan practices permanent employment, and government cooperates with business, and not only does the country grow at a faster rate than we do, but Japanese companies beat us in our own markets. Japanese practices cannot work, yet they do. Japan violates our common sense. How can we deal with a people whose actions do not make common sense?

The Japanese really are different from us. The key questions are not whether but how and why they are different. The most common answer is culture: the Japanese just think differently and have different values. Thus, the best way to understand Japan is to study their values and their ways of thinking. This line of research has a long and distinguished lineage, but chapter 2 presents arguments that play down cultural explanations. While differences in culture are no doubt important, many cultural explanations amount to no more than saying that they

3

do things differently because that's the way they are. This is not an explanation; it is an admission of ignorance. Chapter 3 offers an alternative concept of culture as common sense. Chapters 4 and 5 apply this concept and attempt to make American common sense of permanent employment and government-business cooperation. The goal is to explain these two phenomena in ways that Americans can understand without resorting to mystical cultural explanations.[1] The basic thesis of this book is that Japan can be understood using the same theories that help us understand other industrial democracies.

I am a comparative political scientist. Comparativists are uncomfortable with uniqueness: if something is unique, it cannot be compared and is, therefore, beyond our ken. Thus, I am biased against finding uniqueness; were it there, I would be unlikely to see it. There is an old and continuing battle among social scientists about the best way to study other countries. Area specialists strive for a deep understanding of a single country by immersion in its history and culture. Comparativists use each country as an example and try to explain all relevant examples. I am in the latter camp. Readers are thus forewarned of my basic bias and must judge for themselves whether my arguments are convincing.

Most readers are probably less interested in my intellectual than in my political biases. There is another battle going on in Japanese studies, between the Japan apologists and the Japan bashers. Most of the popular literature on Japan portrays it as either a heaven on earth, where people cooperate out of the basic goodness of their hearts, or as a hellish place in which massive social pressures force people into lives of conformity and quiet desperation. Many of my students come to classes about Japan convinced that it is either heaven or hell, although some are confused about which. I give them the decidedly unromantic answer that it is a normal country with normal people living in it.

While few Japan scholars can be identified as either pure bashers or pure apologists, everything recently written about Japan is attacked as either bashing or apology. No matter what one writes about Japan, one of the first questions asked will be, How does this affect the debate over U.S.-Japan relations?

Some will search the study for signs of bashing, others for evidence of apology. Some will find results that bash Japan, others results that support Japan. The degree to which the politics of trade frictions has invaded academia is sad and alarming.

This political scrutiny often revolves around certain key phrases, assumed to be code words for one's hidden agenda. This book takes as one of its goals the increase of American understanding of Japan. The call for greater understanding is often a call for acceptance of Japanese arguments and is thus seen as a code word for apology. The Japanese themselves tend to equate understanding with acceptance: If Americans just understood why we do things the way we do, they would not ask us to change. Please understand us, often means, Please do not ask us to change our system.

Although I am interested in increased understanding, I do not equate understanding with acceptance. America has made many demands on Japan over the last several years, and Japan has acceded to most of them. However, the results have not lived up to American expectations. Although many have come to the conclusion that Japan works differently from the rest of the world, or that the Japanese change things on paper without changing things in practice, I argue that these conclusions are wrong. We simply do not understand how economies like Japan's work. Understanding how Japan works should allow us to devise more effective demands. I am interested in increasing understanding; but better understanding should produce better policies on both sides of the Pacific. Better policy does not necessarily mean less conflict, but it should mean less conflict over symbolic issues. Informed conflict should prove more useful and less frustrating to both sides. Compromises that work become easier to attain when negotiators base their demands on accurate assessments of the realities of both countries.

By understanding the Japanese economy, we can also learn more about how economies in general work and devise better ways of dealing with our own economic problems. We can learn from Japan. It may be foolish to try to copy Japanese practices simply and directly, but understanding another economy should prove helpful in designing economic policies under any circumstances. At the very minimum, we can lengthen the list of realistic possibilities. At best, we can learn something fundamental about markets, revise our concept of what a market is, and run our own economy better because of this improved understanding. The United States can learn from the Japanese experience. I discuss these lessons in the final chapter.

In sum, I am more interested in understanding than in either bashing or apologizing. I will likely be attacked as a Japan basher because I do not simply spout the Japanese line. To some, the implication that there is a Japanese line amounts to Japan bashing. I hope (and expect that) I will also be attacked as an apologist. I would hate this book to be categorized as either simple bashing or simple apology. The only worse outcome would be to be ignored.

Japan: A Strange and Wondrous Country?

Japan is a country like any other; we can understand Japan by comparing it to other industrial democracies. Over the years, most scholars, both Japanese and Western, have argued that Japan is a unique country, sui generis, a country unlike any other. This argument is back in vogue, as indicated by the sales of books like *The Enigma of Japanese Power* by Karl van Wolferen.[2] Why has the idea of Japanese uniqueness been so popular for so long? One reason is that there are a lot of things about Japan that really are different. However, there are at least two errors that lead to overemphasizing the differences: the tendency to compare Japan only to the United States and the tendency to compare Japanese reality to Western ideals instead of Western realities.

Comparing Japan and the United States

Because a special relationship has existed between Japan and the United States since the end of World War II, there has been a strong tendency to compare the two. Unfortunately, on many dimensions Japan and the United States are the two most different of all industrial democracies.[3] When the differences are noted, the usual conclusion is that Japan is a strange and wondrous country. More often than not, however, the proper conclusion is that Japan is fairly normal, while the United States is strange. In the comparative politics of industrial democracies, Japan has usually been ignored, and America has been the outlier. People who study Western Europe and North America must deal with American exceptionalism.[4] When Japan is compared to both the United States and Western European countries, Japan and the United States appear at far ends of the spectrum, with Western European countries in between but much closer to Japan. On many dimensions, Japan would be a normal European country, but the United States is different, a country not quite like any other.

Let us begin with the simplest possible example. How large is Japan? Ask any Japanese (or any American student of Japanese studies) to describe Japan and the first phrase out of his/her mouth is likely to be, "a small island nation."[5] The phrase has become something of a mantra, repeated by the Japanese to themselves and to foreigners at every opportunity. No matter what question one asks about Japan, the reply is likely to begin, "First, you must understand that Japan is a small island nation." The evidence for the "island nation" part of this orthodoxy is indisputable, but is Japan really small?

Let us compare ten major industrial democracies: Australia, Great Britain, Canada, France, West Germany (the Federal Republic of Germany), Italy, Japan, the Netherlands, Sweden, and the United States. If these nations are ranked from the largest in land area to the smallest, where will Japan fall? Most students, both Japanese and American, guess next to last, ahead only of the Netherlands. Actually, Japan is just a bit smaller than France and Sweden and is significantly larger than Great Britain, Germany, and Italy. If ranked by population (or GNP for that matter), Japan is second after the United States and about twice as large as Great Britain, France, Germany, or Italy. These facts are displayed graphically in figure 1-1. If there is one country in this figure that is off the scale, it is the United States. Australia and Canada have the land area of the United States, but the United States has about twice the population of Japan and four times the population of the major European nations. Japan is small only in comparison to the United States. *Being smaller than the United States makes Japan a perfectly normal country.* The United States is in a league of its own.

Figure 1-1: Is Japan a Small Country?

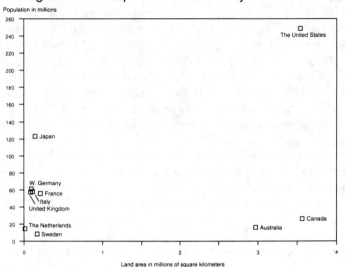

Compared to the other industrial democracies of the world, Japan is a rather large country. Delete the United States, Canada, and Australia, and figure 1-1 becomes figure 1-2. Compared to the major countries of Western Europe, Japan is a big country, roughly the size of a unified Germany.[6] When Germany was reunited, the media were fearful about how this new "large" nation would affect the balance of power in the world. It turns out that "little" Japan is bigger than "big" Germany.

Why do the Japanese insist on describing their country as a small nation? Indeed, after hearing this demonstration in class, many Japanese students still begin their final papers or essay questions with "One must remember that Japan is a small island nation."[7] The French, Germans, and Italians do not describe themselves as small nations. There are at least three more reasons, beyond the tendency to compare themselves to the United States, that the Japanese think of Japan as a small country: history, geographical location, and U.S.-Japan trade frictions.

I like to ask students when Japan became a small island nation. Most answer that it has been so from the beginning of

Figure 1-2: Japan as a European Country

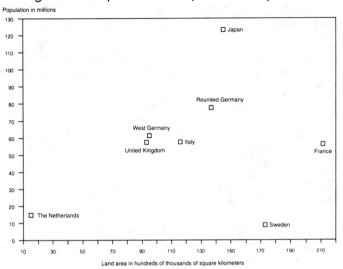

Population in millions

Land area in hundreds of thousands of square kilometers

time. Actually, only since their defeat in World War II have the Japanese described themselves as a small island nation. Until that time, they had belonged to the Japanese Empire, or Greater Japan (Dai-Nippon), and thought of themselves as one of the great powers. They were more likely to compare themselves to Western European nations than to the United States and knew they were bigger than most of those countries. Japan became a small island nation by losing the war. First, by losing the empire Japan became geographically smaller. More important was the psychological impact of losing and returning to the home islands. Great Britain, though it won the war, lost its empire after the war; they also complain of being "little" Britain.

A second reason is geographical location. When Western Europeans look at a map of their environs, they see other nations of comparable size. Japan's neighbors — China, Russia, the United States, Canada, and Australia — are immense relative to Japan. In this company Japan is geographically small, though it still has a large population and is an economic power. In terms of the international relations of the Pacific rim, Japan is some-what justified in thinking of itself as a small country. In par-ticular, Japan is much smaller than its major trading partner and the focus of its foreign policy, the United States.

Often the "small island nation" refrain is meant to deflect U.S. demands for greater burden sharing in international rela-tions. The United States stresses GNP and considers Japan an economic superpower of whom much can be expected. The Japanese stress land area, arguing that one cannot ask too much of "a small island nation." Whatever the merits of this rhetori-cal skirmish in the trade war, from the perspective of com-parative politics, Japan is by no means a small nation. It is quite a normal size. The outlier here is not Japan, but the United States. The United States is a huge country.

If one were to extend the "small island nation" mantra, the next adjective to be added would have to be "homogeneous." Japan *is* a remarkably homogeneous nation (though less so than Korea), and many Japanese leaders seem inordinately pleased with this fact.[8] Most of the people who live in Japan are Japa-nese in language, culture, race, and almost any other way one can think of. However, one should also ask when Japan be-came a homogeneous nation. The usual response is, from the beginning of time. However, prewar Japan was an empire. While clear distinctions were maintained between the Japanese rulers and the non-Japanese ruled, many foreigners lived in Japan, and many Japanese lived abroad. The Japanese islands became ethnically homogeneous after World War II, when the Japa-nese living abroad were forced to return to the home islands, and many of the Koreans and Chinese living in Japan were sent back to their own countries. Moreover, prewar Japan was a class society with large gaps between rich and poor. The flat income distribution and other factors that have produced a nation of "salarymen" with very small differences among the classes are also postwar phenomena.

Another popular image of Japan is as a safe, law-abiding nation, perhaps because of its homogeneity. Often, the implica-tion is that the Japanese are just nicer than we are. While it is currently true that Japan is a safe country, it is true primar-ily in contrast to the United States. Again, it is not Japan but the United States that is the strange country. Murder and robbery rates for several industrial democracies are plotted in figure 1-3. As one might expect, Japan is one of, if not the, safest countries in the world, but the United States is by far the most dangerous of the industrial democracies. American murder rates would look even worse if the American data included attempted, as well as actual, murders. America has more actual murders per hundred thousand people than most countries have attempted murders. Japan has little violent crime, but in this it is not that different from Great Britain or the Netherlands. There is little reason to focus on the question of why Japan has so little crime. The big question is why a rich nation like the United States has so much.

If the Japanese are such a peaceful people, who raped Nanking? Who bombed Pearl Harbor? These questions confuse many younger Japanese. The image of Japanese soldiers at war violates their current self-image, because they assume that the

Figure 1-3: Comparing Rates of Violent Crime

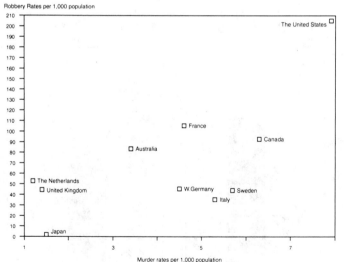

Note: Data are for 1984 except for Italy's and Britain's, which are for 1983. Murder rates are for attempted murder, except for the United States and the Netherlands, which are actual homicides.

Japanese were always as they are now, that Japanese culture is timeless. The Japanese were a violent people before World War II and for many years thereafter. They had serious crime problems, widespread police brutality, labor unrest, and even political assassinations.[9] In fact, American textbooks on Japan written before the mid-1960s often list violence as a primary characteristic of Japanese political culture.[10]

Statistically at least, the Japanese became a peaceful people after 1960. In that year there were serious demonstrations against renewing the security treaty with the United States. If the acts of political violence are averaged over a period of years that includes 1960, Japan will appear to be a relatively violent country. In figure 1-4, the average number of riots per year is given for Great Britain, Italy, and Japan. Averaging these data from 1958 through 1967 makes Japan look fairly normal, a little more violent than Britain and a little less so than Italy. Averaging from 1967 through 1976, however, makes Japan look remarkably peaceful. If we use an average that starts after 1960, Japan will appear to be a nonviolent country. Of course, if we added

Figure 1-4: Average Number of Riots per Year

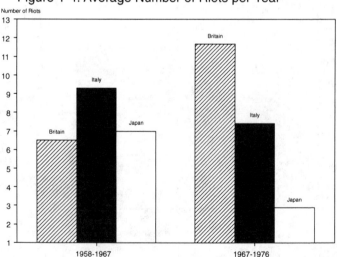

Number of Riots

1958-1967   1967-1976

the United States to this figure, all three nations would look relatively peaceful.[11]

Today Japan is a remarkably nonviolent society, but there are exceptions. The demonstrations against the construction of the new international airport at Narita involved violent and dramatic confrontations with the police and extraordinary security is still necessary around the airport.[12] Students often try to deal with these contradictions by saying that they "have a capacity for violence." Indeed, Japanese are violent at some times and in some places but not in others. Japanese are human; they are sometimes violent. List up all the countries in the world that have *not* committed atrocities in wartime. If you have any countries on your list, you need to study a bit more history. People (including the Japanese) tend to be violent in wartime.

Another suggested indication that the Japanese are just nicer than we are is that they do not sue each other. Americans use the courts more than the Japanese do. Again, this has been true primarily since the end of World War II, because "historically the Japanese have been quite litigious."[13] It is also true only relative to the United States. "That Norway or Sweden say have lower litigation rates than Japan is beside the point; the only external point of reference that counts is the United States."[14] Why are Japan and the United States different? The most common answer is that Americans like to sue and the Japanese do not. Do Americans really like to sue? Why is it that a joke made at the expense of lawyers always gets a laugh?[15] Most Americans do not like courts and lawyers, do not like to sue, and think that one of the United States's biggest problems is a surplus of lawyers. Americans sue not because they like it but because in the United States there is no other way to get things done. Similarly, the Japanese reluctance to sue is not rooted in the Japanese psyche but is due to the structure of the courts, the paucity of lawyers, and the availability of more effective alternatives.[16]

Japanese politics is often considered unique because there has been one party in power since 1955, and conservatives have ruled continuously since 1949. If the same party always wins, is Japan really a democracy? While this is a serious question, a great deal of the contrast between Japan and Western democracies is exaggerated.[17] First of all, Japan is a parliamentary regime without a directly elected president. If America had no president, its electoral history would look remarkably likes Japan's. In the United States in the postwar period, the Republicans have controlled the House of Representatives only twice, from 1947 to 1949 and from 1953 to 1955. In Japan, the Socialists have been represented in a government only once, from 1947 through 1949. The opposition has controlled the legislature twice as often in the United States than in Japan, for four years compared to two years — hardly an impressive difference. The Reagan revolution was unable to overturn Democratic control of the lower house but was able to get a Republican majority in the Senate for six years, from 1981 to 1987. The opposition in Japan also won a majority in the upper house in 1989, and it may well hold on for six years.

The significant difference is not in what the electorate has done but in the structure of government. Controlling the lower house in Japan means controlling the national government. In local government, where the Japanese have a presidential type of system, they have regularly voted out conservative governors and mayors and elected the opposition. It is simply harder to change the majority of a legislative body than to change a directly elected chief executive. Comparing the U.S. Congress with the Japanese Diet, we find more similarities than differences.

Japan's Liberal Democratic party (LDP) does not hold the world record for longevity in office. The Swedish Socialist party (SAP) ruled from 1936 to 1976, while the LDP has been in power only since 1955. More important, the LDP came within a hair's breadth of losing in 1976, exactly when the SAP did lose. The postwar electoral results for these two parties are shown in figures 1-5 and 1-6. The first thing to note is the greater volatility of the Japanese numbers. The LDP percentage of the vote ranges from 41.8 percent in 1976 to 57.8 percent in 1958 and fluctuates widely. The SAP vote ranges from 42.7 percent in 1976 to 50.1 percent in 1968, and the trends are much smoother. The second point is the greater gap between the percentage of votes and the percentage of seats in Japan, represented by the gap between the two lines. Both parties are overrepresented, as are most large parties around the world, but

Figure 1-5: Japan's LDP Since 1958

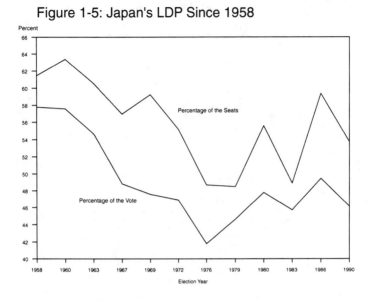

the LDP gets a bigger advantage than does the SAP. Most important, however, the evidence indicates that in 1976 Japanese voters were madder at the LDP than Swedish voters were mad at the SAP. The LDP got 42 percent of the vote, while the SAP got 43 percent. The LDP lost five percentage points, while the SAP only lost one. The LDP lost twenty-two seats, the SAP only four. The LDP managed to hold onto power because Japan's electoral system favors the largest party more than Sweden's does. The difference is not in the intentions of the voters but in the way votes are translated into seats. The 1976 elections in Japan and Sweden are most impressive in their similarity, the major difference being that the LDP was luckier. A comparison of Japan's electoral history with that of other industrial democracies indicates that there is no need to create a special category for Japan.

There are many examples of this pattern of comparing Japan only to the United States, finding that these two countries are indeed quite different, and mistakenly concluding that Japan is a strange country. For example, Japanese texts stress the

Figure 1-6: Sweden's SAP Since 1958

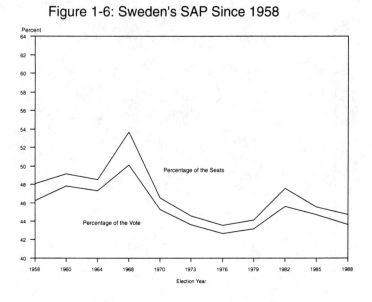

degree to which the country is centralized. It is, indeed, more centralized than the United States, but most of the things Japanese critics of centralization complain about are perfectly normal in Western Europe.[18] Japan is often described as a country with a weak legislative branch and a strong bureaucracy. Again, Japan is a normal country, but the United States is different. The United States is virtually the only country in which the legislature still exercises many of its lawmaking functions.[19] The United States is also the only major industrial democracy that does not have an institutionalized elite bureaucracy; it is the only industrial democracy with "a government of strangers."[20]

It is not difficult to explain why the Japanese tend to compare their country exclusively to the United States. Since the end of World War II, Japan and the United States have been locked into an intense relationship. The United States occupied Japan and tutored it in democracy. It was hard to avoid taking the United States as the standard by which Japan should be judged. Both American and Japanese scholars have often failed to extend the comparison beyond the two countries. Progress is being made slowly. Nevertheless, the basic conclusion of broader comparisons is clear: on many dimensions, Japan is similar to Western European nations, though very different from the United States. Japan and the United States are poles apart, but the strange nation is the United States more often than Japan.

Comparing Japanese Realities to Western Models

The second major error leading us to think of Japan as a strange and wondrous nation is the tendency to compare Japan to Western ideals instead of Western reality.[21] Many Japanese have an image of American democracy that comes right out of our high school civics textbooks. Americans tutored the Japanese in democracy, and it seemed to follow that Americans must actually practice what they preach. The Occupation played its part in perpetuating this myth: for example, the film, *All the King's Men*, about corrupt Louisiana politics was kept out of Japan. The following stories illustrate the massive misunderstanding of American politics (and democratic politics in general) that has persisted in Japan.

A Japanese student taking my course on Japanese politics rebelled when I argued that Japan is not unique and that Japanese democracy is not that different from our own. She protested that Japanese politicians *say* one thing but *do* something else and sometimes actually *lie*. Of course, the American students burst out in raucous laughter. My Japanese student was surprised to learn that the idea that politicians lie is one of the basic pieces of American common sense about politics.[22]

The American students expected to hear some secret about Japan. They were also resisting my arguments and were waiting to hear the real story from a real Japanese. Instead they got a universal fact about democratic politics. It was as if the student had said, "The Japanese are really fundamentally different from the Americans. Most Japanese only have *one* nose!"

Even the Japanese who have lived in the United States have an amazing ability to believe what they learned in high school and college instead of what they see around them. One Japanese friend who lived for several years in Alabama insisted that Japanese politics was inestimably more backward than American politics. We then witnessed George Wallace's final guber-natorial campaign. Because of the historical significance of the event, my friend read the local papers regularly and followed the campaign closely. His conclusion is that American politics is clearly more backward than Japanese politics. More impor-tant, the similarities outweigh the differences. Most everything he saw looked perfectly familiar.

Non-Japanese also tend to compare Japanese realities to Western ideals instead of Western realities. An excellent example is van Wolferen's critique of the Liberal Democratic party:

> This group of politicians is now called the Liberal Democratic Party (LDP) – a total misnomer . . . for a coalition of *habatsu*, politi-cal cliques. It has no party organization to speak of amongst the grass roots, and no generally agreed upon mechanism to regulate succession to its leadership, nor does it stand for any identifiable political principles. . . . It is thus scarcely a political party at all in the accepted Western sense.[23]

While I disagree only a bit with this description of the LDP, by the same definition, America has no political parties at all.[24] Whereas Western Europe traditionally has had stronger, more ideological parties, the most successful parties have evolved toward less coherent catchall organizations.[25] In fact, when the LDP is described as a predominant, catchall party, students of comparative politics immediately recognize the syndrome and understand the basic characteristics of the LDP. Often van Wolferen accurately describes Japan, but the West he compares it with exists only in old textbooks, not in current reality.

Many Japanese would be quite comfortable with van Wolf-eren's critique. They are surprised to find that many Western political parties are more like the LDP than like conventional Western models of political parties. I was asked by one Japa-nese student about the ideologies of the Democrats and the Republicans. He repeated the standard descriptions of Demo-crats more or less in favor of big government and helping the weaker parts of society, while the Republicans tend to want less government and favor big business. I was impressed. The Japanese student had done as well as most American students in defining the parties' ideologies. But the Japanese student was shocked when I told him that he was right. He knew there must be more. He was certain that American political parties must have more coherent ideologies, because everyone always criticizes the LDP for not having one.

The Japanese political system is plagued by recurrent scandals but the Japanese are surprised to learn that the American system has problems as well. The Japanese seem to think that pork barrel politics was invented in Japan. Tanaka Kakuei is a famous Japanese politician. He made his way to the top by building a political machine in his district to guarantee his reelection, no matter what else happened, and then maneuvered skillfully (and sometimes deceitfully) in the Diet (the national legislature).[26] In Japan I am often asked, "Surely there are no politicians like Tanaka in the United States, are there?" In response, I suggest that one good way of understanding Tanaka Kakuei is to read a biography of Lyndon Baines Johnson.[27] The parallels are striking. My audience next offers examples of more disreputable conduct. Surely there has never been a politician elected to the U.S. Congress who had connections to organized crime, they say. Actually, I would bet that the percentage is higher in the United States, though I cannot imagine how one could collect the data to test such a hypothesis.

Tanaka Kakuei was convicted of corruption charges but remained in the Diet during his appeal and, in fact, continued to exercise a great deal of power behind the scenes. Surely American voters never reelect someone who has been convicted of a crime, the Japanese assume. Of course we do, and for precisely the same reasons. In the United States between 1968 and 1978, seventy-one congressional candidates were charged with corruption.[28] Of these, 75 percent were elected. Several decided not to run, a phenomenon that also occurs in Japan, though it is seldom noted. Several others failed to win renomination in the primary (there are no primaries in the Japanese system). Almost all who had been charged lost a significant number of votes, though seldom enough to unseat an established incumbent. This is also normal in Japan. In the 1990 election, eleven of the fifteen candidates involved in the Recruit scandal lost votes, though only one lost his seat.[29] It is widely believed in Japan that left-wing candidates are more severely punished for corruption than are conservatives;[30] the American data support this hypothesis, accused Democrats losing almost twice as many votes as accused Republicans.

The frequent reelection of Japanese candidates charged with corruption is often taken to mean that the electorate is not much concerned with corruption. However, in each of the major scandal elections, the ruling party or coalition has suffered serious losses. Individuals may seem invulnerable, but political parties are clearly hurt by scandals. In part, this is due to the localist bias of the Japanese electoral system. For example, Tanaka Kakuei was an extremely unpopular man in 1976 — everywhere, that is, except in his own Niigata Third District. The local voters rose up to defend their representative against attacks by the national media. It is not hard to imagine American voters acting exactly the same way. Tanaka's fate is often compared to that of Richard Nixon, but Tanaka could not have won a nationwide presidential election any more than Nixon could have after Watergate. Fortunately for Tanaka, he did not have to. Attention to district needs insulates politicians from electoral tides everywhere.[31] It may well be that the Japanese electoral system favors such candidates more than other systems, but Japanese voters react very much like other voters when faced with corrupt politicians.

The Japanese are surprised to learn that American attitudes toward money and politics are similar to their own. The *Asahi Shimbun* newspaper conducted a poll of Americans and Japanese on the issue of corruption.[32] Both responded that the biggest ethical problem in politics was money (Japanese 62 percent, Americans 54 percent). Lying was the second most commonly cited problem in both countries (Japanese 35 percent, Americans 33 percent). The biggest difference was that some Americans were most worried about alcohol (7 percent) and others were most worried about sex scandals (4 percent). No Japanese cited either of these problems as primary. When asked if they thought that money influenced the outcome of elections, 82 percent of the Japanese and 84 percent of Americans answered in the affirmative. When asked if they thought that companies that contribute money to campaigns have undue influence, 86 percent of the Japanese and 81 percent of the Americans said yes. Many Japanese were surprised to learn that Americans are just as worried about corruption as they are, and Americans often conveniently forget the realities of American politics when discussing democracy in Japan.

Japan has, without question, a major problem with corruption. However, there has been little comparative study done of corruption in politics.[33] Impressionistically, one tends to rank Japan with Italy, as democracies in which corruption is rampant; but studies of corruption in Italy reveal many things that could not happen in Japan, most notably the level of violence.[34] France has also been characterized as a country "where scandals emerge quite frequently but where those implicated suffer very few serious or lasting consequences."[35] In fact an insider trading scandal occurred in France in 1989 similar to the Japanese Recruit scandal.[36] The Flick scandal in Germany would be familiar to the Japanese: allegations of bribery and corruption were made in 1976, and the trial ended only in 1987. The defendants in this case were convicted of tax evasion but cleared of the corruption charges, because "under-the-table contributions had been tolerated for so long, a blanket judgement of illegality would have convicted almost the entire governing class."[37] One difficulty in comparing the degrees of corruptions in different countries is that styles of corruption vary so widely among countries. Japanese scandals tend to involve money, but Japan has had neither the sex scandals common in Britain nor anything like the constitutional scandal of Watergate in the United States.

In the Lockheed scandal, the Japanese courts performed relatively well, convicting a former prime minister and giving him a stiff sentence. The process seemed unconscionably long to observers but may well have been reasonably quick by international standards. The Japanese failure lay in the inability of the Japanese Diet or the Liberal Democratic party to purge themselves of Tanaka Kakuei's influence, even after he had been indicted and convicted. The facts of the recent Recruit scandal in Japan are remarkably similar to the Keating savings and loan scandal in the United States. The stories are similar, but the parameters are different: America had the Keating Five, while Japan had the Recruit Multitude. Similarly, the Nomura securities scandal in Japan and the Salomon Brothers scandal in the United States follow essentially the same script, though on a larger scale.[38]

Until we have comparative studies (as opposed to studying one country at a time), we will not really know whether corruption is greater in Japan than in other democracies or to what extent Japanese voters differ in their response to corruption. What is clear from the information available now, however, is that the differences between Japan and the other democracies of the world are not so great as to require creating a separate category for Japan.

Every once in a while, a Japanese will turn to a foreigner and ask, "Do you really believe Japan is a democracy?" indicating that the Japanese himself does not really think so. This is usually interpreted by the foreigner as a dropping of the pretense and, therefore, as convincing evidence that Japan is not really what it seems. This way of thinking always yields negative conclusions about a country: if a Japanese says something good about his country, it is pretense; if he says something bad about his country it is the real scoop, the behind-the-scenes story. These rules of evidence always lead to the worst possible conclusions.[39] Actually, the Japanese who admits that Japan is not a real democracy is acknowledging that it does not look much like the American civics textbook description of a democracy. Using these standards we would find that the world contains no democracies at all. *Failing to live up to a high school textbook standard of democracy makes Japan a perfectly normal country.* If we use a more reasonable, comparative standard, Japan is an industrial democracy much like those in Western Europe and North America.[40]

Japanese ignorance of other democracies may actually be a danger to Japanese democracy. The idea that the civics textbook description of democracy is possible and widely practiced elsewhere makes it easy for the Japanese to conclude that democracy is impossible in Japan and that they must opt for some form of authoritarianism. Yayama Taro sees parallels between the handling of the Recruit scandal and the prewar Teijin affair, which was used as part of an attack on political parties in general.[41] Comparative study of other countries could put Japan's problem in a more realistic perspective.

Fighting the Myth of Japanese Uniqueness

It is frustrating to argue against the myth of Japanese uniqueness. Both the Japanese and Americans like the myth and resist giving it up. American students seem to prefer to see Japan as a country that is either heaven or hell. A Japan that is heaven is a convenient tool for criticizing America's shortcomings. A Japan that is hell is a convenient scapegoat for those same shortcomings. Arguments between the heaven faction and the hell faction can become righteous and heated. Much of the original attraction of studying Japan is its uniqueness. We enjoy the romance of the exotic and inscrutable East.[42] If Japan is a country like any other, then why spend all that time studying such a difficult language?

The Japanese also enjoy being considered unique. All countries like to think that they are special. It is basic human psychology to distinguish us from them. Nationalism demands that each nation have a unique character, and politicians work hard to nurture that belief. The Japanese, however, often go to extremes in defending their uniqueness. The Japanese refuse to believe that anyone not born and raised in Japan can actually speak their language. Foreigners who speak Japanese are often stared at as if they were Mr. Ed, the talking horse. The Japanese also have trouble with people who look Japanese but do not speak the language. In the film, *Living on Tokyo Time,* people cannot believe that a second-generation Japanese-American does not like *manjū* ("All Japanese like *manjū*") and that he cannot speak Japanese. The Japanese often assume that any Japanese understands everything Japanese better than any foreigner, no matter how long the foreigner has studied it. An American who has studied Japanese elections for ten years is assumed to know less about Japanese politics than the average Japanese taxi driver.

The goal of comparative politics is to produce valid cross-national generalizations. Most Japanese seem to think that the only possible reason to compare Japan to other nations is to find out how Japan is unique, to discover Japan's "special characteristics" (*Nihon no tokuchō*). They are always surprised by my response. "Special characteristics? I am sorry, I haven't given that any thought." If I am in a bad mood and unwilling to live up to Japanese standards of politeness, I will go on to say, "I am not interested in Japan's special characteristics. I am interested in such things as the relationship between central and local governments and electoral systems. I study Japan to learn about politics, not to discover Japan's special characteristics."

Japan clearly falls into the class of industrial democracies and can profitably be compared to other such countries. There is no need to create a special category for Japan. It is a normal country. A factor analysis intended to determine which countries are most alike, using almost any political, economic, or social data, would situate Japan in Western Europe, perhaps a bit north of France and just south of Germany. In fact, Arend Lijphart has analyzed the industrial democracies of the world in this way and finds Japan to be quite similar to Italy.[43]

CHAPTER TWO

Culture as Common Sense

Why are Japanese so different from Americans? The natural, even knee-jerk, reaction to this question is that the Japanese *think* differently from us; it must be something inside their heads. However, psychologists have shown that, in explaining the behavior of others, we tend to overestimate the effect of others' values and underestimate the effect of their situations.[1] This is known as the "fundamental attribution error," defined as "the tendency to attribute behavior exclusively to the actor's dispositions and to ignore powerful situational determinants of the behavior."[2] I wish to make a parallel argument that, in analyzing other nations, we tend to overestimate differences in values and underestimate differences in situations. We need to pay less attention to the way the Japanese think and more attention to the context of their behavior, the circumstances to which they are reacting.

The basic experience that convinces us that the Japanese (or any other people) are different from us is observing some Japanese behavior pattern and thinking that, in a similar situation, an American would behave differently. There are three possible explanations for this response. First, we may be correct. The Japanese do not think like us, and an American would act differently in a similar situation. The second possibility is that we do not understand the situation fully. If we did, we would know that an American would act very much like a Japanese in that situation. Japanese behavior would then make American common sense. My basic contention is that there is a great

25

deal more to be found in the second category than the first. A third possibility, rare but important, is that we do not understand Americans; that is, our model of American behavior is mistaken. Normally, Americans have very good information on American behavior. However, when our models of our own behavior are challenged, we can better understand both Americans and basic human nature. Whenever we find ourselves thinking that, in a similar situation, an American would do something completely different, we should consider each of these three possibilities and not leap to the conclusion that the difference lies in some categorical difference in thinking.

The Fundamental Attribution Error

Our tendency to attribute causation to another's personal preferences is a powerful one. I have had several experiences in which I found myself suffering because I had committed the fundamental attribution error.

When I was first doing research in Japan I was quite confident that I understood the Japanese. I had read all the best books about Japanese culture. I was ready to adjust my behavior up to a point but was unwilling to completely abandon my own values and personality. One of my declarations of personal independence involved umbrellas. I was raised in the Midwest, and midwesterners think of umbrellas as unmanly;[3] however, as a concession to Japanese culture, I wore a suit and carried an umbrella. As I left my apartment on the way to my first appointment I noticed a mist in the air. The ground was wet, but no drops of rain were falling. Nevertheless, all the Japanese had their umbrellas up. I immediately concluded that Japanese are wimps. I also knew from my studies that Japanese are conformist: one person puts up an umbrella and all will follow suit (like sheep, you know). I decided that there was no reason for me to participate in this particular cultural phenomenon. I walked to the station, ostentatiously carrying my umbrella folded at my side. When I reached the station I found that the shoulders of my suit were drenched. The mist, which I had so lightly dismissed, was heavier than anything I had ever seen in Indiana. Even though there were no raindrops in the air, an umbrella would have been an excellent idea.

My umbrella experience came to mind again several years later, when I moved to Alabama. I was driving along a four-lane highway when it began to rain. Most of the Alabama drivers slowed down and moved to the right lane. I immediately concluded that southerners are wimps who do not know how to drive in the rain. Hoosiers like myself are not afraid of a little rain. I confidently pulled out into the left lane and began to pass all the slower-moving vehicles. Then the rain really began to fall. Visibility dropped to ten feet, and the water on the road got deep enough to make driving hazardous. I decided that I would slow down and get into the right lane like everyone else.

In both these cases I not only made the fundamental attribution error but also made it immediately, without hesitation, and with absolute confidence. I assumed that people acted as they did because their values were different from my own; it had to be something inside their heads. In both cases, I was completely mistaken. They acted as they did because of the way rain falls in that area. The cause of their behavior was not inside their heads but in the climate. As a foreigner, I did not understand the circumstances and acted stupidly. Fortunately, in these two cases I learned quickly, because the feedback from my errors was obvious and immediate: I got wet. Learning would have been difficult to avoid. In other cases it is easy to continue acting stupid much longer.

Once I had made the connection between these two experiences, I recalled several other instances of similar errors. Driving through the American southwest, I was amused to see a warning sign beside a little dip in the road: Watch for Flash Floods. I thought, Now these are really cautious people. The humidity is zero; no clouds in the sky; and all the plant life looks parched. They get a heavy rain once every other ice age but they put up a sign, *just in case!* It turns out, of course, that flash floods are reasonably common in the area. One should worry about the rain up in the mountains, not in the immediate area.

When I taught in Seattle, I was prepared. After relating my umbrella story, I told my students there that I already knew something about their culture, their deepest values, without ever talking to them. I knew that the idea that umbrellas are only for wimps would never sell in Seattle. The students were quick to understand that my guess was based not on a thorough analysis of northwestern literature, nor on psychological testing of a random sample of Seattle residents, but on a map showing average annual rainfall in the Seattle area.

I am now more careful. I make an effort to avoid the fundamental attribution error. Whenever I see people doing something I do not understand, I try to think about both the situation and their values. In general, any given behavior can be explained by the interaction of individual preferences and the particular situation. At an aggregate level of analysis, culture represents the values shared by a group, and structure represents the relatively constant or repetitive situations people find themselves in. Sometimes the situation dominates and the question of values hardly enters the equation. Norton Long provides the classic example of analysis based on situation: "If we know the game being played is baseball and that X is a third baseman, by knowing his position and the game being played we can tell more about X's activities on the field than we could if we examined X as a psychologist or a psychiatrist."[4] It also would not help much to know whether the player is Japanese or American, at least until the umpire makes a close call, and the American third baseman reacts with much greater animation than his Japanese counterpart would.

Other behavior is dominated by personal preferences — vanilla or chocolate ice cream, for example. Much of social science research is designed to explain why people make different choices in exactly the same situation: why a consumer chooses a red or a blue car, why a voter chooses the Democratic or Republican presidential candidate, or how a Supreme Court judge decides to vote on a particular case.[5] When the situation is held constant, one naturally and properly focuses on values to explain behavior. Because so much of our research holds the situation constant, we tend to assume that situations are similar when they are actually quite different.[6] For example, we tend to assume that working for a company is essentially the same experience, whether the company is Japanese or American, and therefore any difference in Japanese behavior must be caused by different values. In fact, Americans working for a Japanese company often behave much like the Japanese, and Japanese workers in an American company act more like Americans. The working environment and conditions of promotion are different, and people adjust to the situations — the incentive structure — in which they find themselves. In comparative cross-national research, more attention must be paid to how situations differ. This will explain more, reduce our emphasis on culture, and increase our emphasis on structure.

The best single example I know of comes from Susan Hanley. She argues that many things Americans find strange about Japanese behavior make good sense when one understands that the high price of land in Japan changes living styles. It is a matter not of preferences but of the choices available. Thus,

> the poorest and the richest families are the least likely to have three generations in a household, the poorest for lack of space and the richest because they can afford to live separately. It is the struggling middle class that double up with grandparents. Were three-generation families a cultural characteristic valued by the Japanese as a whole, one would not expect to find this discrepancy in the statistics.[7]

Those people who have the most options do not choose a traditional lifestyle. Similarly,

> whereas the designs for detached houses available for families at the upper end of the income scale are similar in principle to Western houses, designs for small urban rental units are very different. Despite the fact that these are designed for younger Japanese in metropolitan areas — those who would be expected to live in the most modern of lifestyles — they retain many features of the premodern urban house.[8]

People with modern values often live in traditional homes because they have no choice. If you understand the situation, Japanese life-styles make good common sense.

This abstract discussion of values and situations has practical as well as academic implications. Now, whenever I find myself in a group where everyone else is doing something that confounds my common sense, I tend to go along and ask why later. Nevertheless, there is one other aspect of these experiences that continued to bother me. Why had I made these errors with such great confidence? I was so certain that I *knew* about rain. It was just common sense that mists cannot get you wet and that rain never limits driving visibility for long. I knew these things from my own experience. No one told me. It was obvious. Common sense, it turns out, is a good definition of culture.

Culture as Common Sense

What is culture? One suggested definition is: "The political culture of a society consists of the system of empirical beliefs, expressive symbols, and values which defines the situation in which political action takes place."[9] Where does culture come from? Culture is commonly thought to be a product of socialization. Our culture is passed down from generation to generation by our parents and teachers. While I do not deny that a great deal of what we believe comes from our parents and teachers, my own experiences as a son, student, father, and teacher all lead me to conclude that our most basic beliefs do not come from socialization but from our own experiences.[10]

When someone claims that people get their basic values from their parents and teachers, there is probably a strong wish factor added into the equation. As a parent and teacher, I too would like to believe that I have an enormous effect on my children and students. My experience, however, suggests that my influence is limited. More specifically, whenever my teachings must compete with their own testing of the world they live in, I will almost always lose. Perhaps grade school teachers are able to mold their students; but teaching in college is much more like pulling teeth (and one finds that the teeth one has spent so much time and effort pulling often grow back a few weeks after the class ends).[11]

How effective is socialization? Years of socialization aimed at producing good communists was not particularly effective in Eastern Europe or the Soviet Union. Neither did years of socialization under the right-wing authoritarian governments of Spain and Portugal produce much loyalty to those regimes. In each of these cases, the parties in power assumed that they had popular support because no one rebelled, and only a few complained. Once the people were allowed to express their opinions freely in an open election, the parties that represented the old regimes were devastated. Do Iraqis demonstrate for their "beloved leader" Saddam Hussein because they support Saddam or because they are afraid not to? We may never know, because the likelihood of a free election in Iraq is virtually nil. However, we do know that all the effort the Japanese government spent trying to make State Shinto the national religion had little effect on the actual practices and beliefs of the populace.[12]

The idea that socialization is a matter of passive acceptance by one generation of the ideas and attitudes of the previous generation is another example of overemphasizing inside-the-head variables and underestimating the influence of the environment. My father grew up during the depression. To him, the idea that one should never quit one job without another job waiting is just common sense. He tried his best to pass this piece of wisdom on to his children. But we grew up in the 1960s, when one could always find another job. My father's teaching conflicted with our own experiences. Though we considered his ideas quaint and old-fashioned well into the 1970s, his ideas looked a good deal more modern in the 1980s. If we derive our culture from our parents and teachers, where do generation gaps come from?

Children and students listen to parents and teachers but also rebel against what they have been taught, testing it against reality. Most of what we teach our children comes from our own common sense, and is usually confirmed in the testing process. Societies seldom change rapidly enough to invalidate large parts of one generation's common sense for the next. Some aspects of common sense may even be universal. On the other hand, societies never stop changing. There will always be aspects of one generation's common sense that the next generation finds to be false. Generation gaps are produced in part by the changing situations young people find themselves in. Culture changes; it adjusts to physical, social, economic, and political realities.

It is true that any given reality can be interpreted in many different ways. People do not deal with reality directly but through psychological and cultural screens. An American and a Japanese can see the same reality differently. However, this is a very subtle point. While true that an American and a Japanese do not have identical images of a chair because normal sitting in Japan is on the floor, all Japanese understand the basic functions of a chair and would be unlikely to stand on it. The interpretations of the concept of chair are different, but the differences have few practical implications. It is also true that my desk consists mostly of the empty space between the atomic nucleii and the electrons. This subtle truth does not keep me from setting my coffee cup on the desk in perfect confidence that it will not fall through.

More fundamentally, any interpretation of reality has to make sense. There are limits to the range of interpretations that can be put on any situation. You cannot tell residents of a ghetto that crime does not pay, when the only rich people they see are drug dealers. Though no single interpretation of reality will always dominate, any interpretation, to be accepted, must work in that environment. Even the most thorough propaganda campaign cannot manipulate culture beyond the limits of credibility. The smartest thing ever said about democracy is Lincoln's famous line: "You can fool all the people some of the time; you can fool some of the people all of the time; but you cannot fool all the people all of the time." The power of socialization is limited to those interpretations of reality that can withstand testing against one's personal experience.

If reality — the situation people live in — changes, then culture will change as well, even if parents and teachers continue to teach us exactly what our grandparents were taught. The idea that culture changes violates one of our basic notions of what is meant by culture. We tend to view culture as the unchanging core of a nation's values. This definition of culture makes it a magical, mystical thing. Culture persists, and its component beliefs form a coherent whole. "The concept of political culture thus suggests that the traditions of a society, the spirit of its public institutions, the passions and the collective reasoning of its citizenry, and the style and operating codes of its leaders are not just random products of historical experience but fit together as a part of a meaningful whole and constitute an intelligible web of relations."[13] While there may be some constraints on how widely parts of a culture can vary, to some extent any behavior is appropriate somewhere or sometime in all cultures. Moreover, it is easy to fall into the trap of assuming permanence and consistency, so that the national culture becomes a single entity stretching across time. I have heard historians talk as if an eighth-century poem, a sixteenth-century government document, a statement by a famous person, and a recent newspaper editorial were all equally valid expressions of a culture and, therefore, equally good predictors of the future. This approach will always lead to the prediction that no culture will ever change, and sooner or later, that prediction will prove to be mistaken.

Any student of history should understand that cultures change.[14] I can convince people over the age of forty that culture changes simply by saying, Americans will never buy small cars. Economists said it would depend on the price of gasoline; but we "knew" that, to an American, a car is not simply a means of transportation, it is a symbol of one's personality — particularly for men. Such deeply held cultural values are simply not subject to change. Although we "knew" that Americans would never, under any circumstances, buy small cars, we see small cars all over American roads. The theory has, of course, been disproved by the facts. Culture does change in response to a changed environment.[15]

In fact, the holistic, unchanging, mystical concept of culture is considered a straw man in most academic writing.[16] It is also, however, common among journalists and is the starting point for almost all students of Japanese studies. In some ways this book grew out of an experience I had early in my teaching career. To get the class interested, I began by telling a few funny stories about strange things the Japanese do. The students loved it, but they were swallowing it whole, without thinking. To see how much they would accept without question, I began exaggerating, telling them that the Japanese work hard whether they are paid or not, need only an hour of sleep a night, and do not feel pain as we do. I had hoped to discourage some of their mystical cultural conceptions; but my students diligently continued taking notes.

Everyone is vulnerable to the fundamental attribution error.[17] It is remarkably easy to fall back into the mystical concept of culture as a core of values inside Japanese heads that has been there for centuries, put there by the goddess Amaterasu and somehow passed along genetically to all Japanese, past, present, and future. The fundamental attribution error is such a natural way of thinking that it takes the pedagogical equivalent of a two-by-four across the forehead several times to knock the idea out of students heads. The following section contains my most effective two-by-fours. Chapter 3 presents an alternative way of thinking about culture, but the main purpose of the present chapter is to immunize students against the fundamental cultural attribution error.[18]

Mystical Concepts of Culture

I am not attacking the idea of culture, only mystical conceptions of culture. Culture clearly exists. The Japanese do think differently from Americans. The question is not whether but how and why. Mystical concepts of culture are those in which the mechanism of transmission is left unspecified. Mystical conceptions tend to assume that a nation's culture is eternal and unchanging: if we know what the Japanese were like in 1400, we know what they are like now. Mystical conceptions also assume that there is a cultural core of values that infuse the whole of society: if we understand the Japanese tea ceremony, we know how Japanese politics works, why Japan's economy grew so fast, and why its crime rate is so low.

A mystical concept of culture assumes that it persists over the centuries. One can find examples of remarkably familiar Japanese behavior from many different periods of history. For example, Robert J. Smith has collected "a miscellany of historical instances" in which the Japanese "beat the white man at his own game."[19] His examples are truly impressive. On the other hand, one can also find examples of totally un-Japanese behavior. Japanese visitors to the United States in the 1900s found the secret of American success in the fact that Americans worked so much harder than the Japanese.[20] A prewar Japanese businessman complained that the Japanese have no spirit of cooperation and thus few joint ventures.[21] Finally, one can find examples of remarkably Japanese behavior in other people. A Japanese friend of mine was looking forward to seeing American-style decision making in action during his two years in American universities. What he saw was perfectly familiar Japanese-style consensus decision making.[22] If we look hard enough, we can find every facet of the human experience in the history of any country. If our search is not systematic and comparative, we will simply produce an endless stream of examples. We can select examples that prove that culture persists over the centuries, or we can select other examples that prove that culture does not matter at all. Only systematic comparison and analysis can make sense of the examples.

What of culture persists and what does not? One approach to this question is to assume that the most important aspects of a nation's culture, the core, is somehow eternal. However, in order to fit the whole history of a country under one umbrella, such unchanging core characteristics must be so vague as to be virtually useless. Anything, including the history of all other nations of the world, could also be fitted under the same vague umbrella. *The Dream of the Red Chamber* (Chinese), *The Brothers Karamazov* (Russian), and *To Kill a Mockingbird* (American South) could be presented as Japanese novels from different historical periods, and an unchanging cultural core could be found in these three or any other set of books. A cultural core can always be found, because of the amazing ability of the human mind to find patterns in the most diverse phenomena. But this has nothing to do with the nature of culture.

One result of the search for a cultural core is a set of paradoxical generalizations. Paradoxical generalizations about Japanese culture are particularly common: the Japanese are both violent and passive, loyal and treacherous, rigid and adaptable.[23] Such generalizations are accepted without question by many students of Japanese culture. I find these paradoxical and mystical concepts of culture totally useless. If I know that Japanese are both violent and passive, what do I know? However, useless answers to hard questions seem to sell quite well.[24]

One reason cultural explanations sell so well is that they can explain anything. In the 1940s, we explained why China was underdeveloped and Japan developed by saying that China was Confucian and Japan was not. Now that Korea and Taiwan, like Japan, are experiencing economic success, this success is attributed to the Confucianism shared by all three countries. (Is China no longer Confucian?) Confucianism can explain their economic growth or lack of economic growth. Japan is Confucian when we are explaining similarities with other East Asian nations and non-Confucian when we are explaining differences. On the one hand, we hear arguments that the current economic growth of South Korea cannot be explained without reference to cultural similarities with Japan.[25] On the other hand, one should not expect the merger of the two largest parties in Korea to turn out like the Liberal Democratic party in Japan, because of the vastly different cultural context.[26] When Japan and Korea look similar, it is because their cultures are similar. When Japan and Korea look different, it is because their cultures are different. If the Korean party merger works out better than expected, we will be able to explain, after the fact, that Korean culture is almost the same as the Japanese. Question: Who will win tomorrow's football game? Answer: The team that wants it more. Question: Which team is that? Answer: I will be able to tell you with absolute certainty as soon as the game is over. Question: Are Japanese and Korean cultures similar or different? Answer: Are we trying to explain a similarity or a difference?

Another common way of describing the cultural core is with some untranslatable word in the original language that is the key to understanding a people's behavior. The most famous such words for Japan are *wa* and *amae*. *Wa* is a sense of balance and harmony, perhaps best translated as "teamwork."[27] *Amae* is an emotion that ties two people together in an unequal relationship.[28] Of course, only a Japanese can fully comprehend these terms; they cannot be translated. However, it is suggested that, to the degree we do understand these terms, we will understand every other aspect of Japanese behavior.

These concepts are the social science equivalent of a panacea in medicine (one medicine that cures all diseases) or a philosophers' stone in chemistry (a substance that will turn any base metal into gold). The idea that one key concept can explain many other things has been abandoned in medicine and in chemistry. We should abandon it in the social sciences as well.[29]

The idea of an unchanging cultural core is attractive, both intellectually and politically. Intellectually, the idea seems to offer a key. Politically, it is an effective tool for arguing that "we" are different from "them," a way of creating and sustaining nationalism. As such, cultural arguments tend to get totally out of hand in wartime.[30] Even in peacetime, national self-interest is often quite visible in cultural arguments. "At one time or another in recent years, for example, the Japanese have declared that their snow, intestines, baseballs, and soil all have unique qualities (thus rationalizing import restrictions on skis, beef, and baseball bats, and exclusion of foreign contractors on domestic construction projects)."[31] These arguments have a powerful emotional impact but are often completely illogical. If the Japanese cannot digest beef, there should be no demand for beef in Japan and no need for import restrictions. The most contradictory part of these arguments, however, is the fact that the very people who affirm an eternal core of Japaneseness also worry about how to keep younger Japanese from becoming Westernized.

In the prewar period, Japanese conservatives argued that Japan's beautiful customs made Western-style labor unions and competitive political parties unnecessary. These same people were also appalled at the individualism of Japanese youth. They argued that the youth must be protected from the influence of Western individualism.[32] If there really is an eternal core to Japanese culture, why worry about the younger Japanese changing their values? Many of the proposals to create a uniquely Japanese style of labor relations were copied from Nazi Germany.[33] Retaining Japan's beautiful customs often meant copying Germany more and copying Great Britain less.

More recently, there has been a boom in *Nihonjin-ron* (the theory of Japaneseness) books and articles explaining exactly how and why the Japanese people are unique and unlike any other.[34] At the same time, there is a boom in *shinjinrui* (the new human species) literature, which argues that today's youth are completely different from their forefathers. Ironically, support for the idea that culture can change comes from some of the most enthusiastic promoters of the idea of Japan's cultural uniqueness. In fact, it may be that the Japanese elite has spent more conscious effort trying to shape its culture than have elites in other countries.[35] It is more likely that we underestimate the degree to which all elites everywhere try to shape their national cultures.

I do not wish to imply that all Japanese culture is a product of elite manipulation. Attempts at manipulation are common, but so also are failures: witness the failure of the wartime government to promote Shinto as a national religion.[36] Neither do I wish to imply that all people who argue Japanese uniqueness do so for nationalistic reasons. In fact, the manipulation that occurs is seldom the cynical and devious process that the English term implies. The best single illustration I know comes from John Campbell's experience:

> In the days of the American "war on poverty," I helped organize a U.S.-Japan conference of mostly child psychologists to talk about pre-school education. The Japanese side said there was no need for special "head-start" programs in Japan because it is a middle-class society. An American participant then produced a table buried in the Japanese materials which indicated that the correlation between socioeconomic status and achievement in primary school was almost as strong as the American correlations which had aroused such great concern. (Note that the only measure of status in the survey was "size of house," included apparently because of an interest in space available for studying.) The somewhat abashed response was that Japanese do not like direct questions about their income, and in any case the Ministry of Education, which sponsored the research, did not encourage questions about the relationship between socioeconomic class and school achievement, because Japan is a middle-class society.[37]

There is some manipulation inherent in any government-sponsored research in any country. If Japanese culture really is manipulated more, it is because there are fewer legitimate voices saying anything other than the standard line.

The fact is that culture does change, though slowly. But culture is also a drag on change, a factor resisting change.[38] People do not immediately change their basic ideas about reality in response to a changing environment. People do learn: witness my willingness to use an umbrella when in Japan. But people also refuse to learn, holding onto ideas that are completely out of date: witness the French calvary's repeated attacks on machine-gun nests in World War I, despite the obvious futility of such action. In the aggregate, it may be accurate to say that culture changes at a glacial pace. Much of Japanese culture today will be similar fifty, even a hundred, years from now. However, with respect to any particular aspect of culture, it is more accurate and more useful to say that culture changes at a generational pace.[39] Each new generation tests the received wisdom of its elders and revises those parts that no longer make sense in the changed environment.

Logical Errors of the Cultural Argument

The cultural argument is prone to several errors that either invalidate the argument or reduce it to a response of That's just the way they are.

The most familiar error, stereotyping, is an extremely useful, but often highly misleading, shorthand way of storing information on different groups. We tend to draw a picture of the typical Japanese in our minds based on the available information, however limited. Though stereotypes sometimes accurately depict the average or modal characteristic of a group, they are generally inaccurate predictors of individual opinion or behavior.

The survey of Japanese and Americans' ethical concerns in politics is a good example. Such findings are usually summarized by saying that the Japanese are more concerned about political bribery, Americans about the lifestyles of their politicians. But the figures themselves belie this conclusion: only 8 percent more Japanese than Americans named money as the major ethical problem in politics; and though Americans are more worried, relative to the Japanese, about sexual morality, in fact only one in ten responding Americans voiced this concern. Averages tell us a lot but are still just averages.

Given the information that the Japanese are more concerned

about money in politics and Americans more concerned about sexual morality, students will invariably estimate the differences as much greater than they really are. They generally guess that 95 percent of the Japanese are intensely concerned about money politics and 75 percent of Americans worry about sexual morality in politicians. Thus, by presenting students with only the averages, we tend to pass on stereotypes. Variety is difficult to communicate.[40]

I once met a journalist assigned to do a story on the Japanese moving to the American South. Over lunch he told several funny stories about the Japanese interacting with American blacks. The Japanese tended to take the stereotypes about black people literally, assuming that they all play basketball, drive Cadillacs, and can dance.[41] He gave a practical sociological analysis of the variations in black culture in America and the individual variations that often negate all stereotypes. But he was a bit surprised when I suggested that the American attitudes toward the Japanese are similarly stereotypical. The less we know about a group, the more likely we are to believe the stereotypes.

The second logical error that conceptions of culture are prone to is the $n = k$ problem.[42] The number of cases to be explained is n; the number of explanations is k. When we use one explanation per case, that is, when $n = k$, we can always explain everything. Sweden spends more on welfare than do Japan or the United States. This could be attributed to cultural differences: the Swedes spend a lot because of their unique communitarian culture; the Americans spend little because Americans are individualistic; the Japanese spend little because they believe the family should care for its own. The quality of communitarianism is claimed as the cause of both greater spending in Sweden and lesser spending in Japan; and opposite qualities — individualism, in the United States, and communitarianism, in Japan — manifest the same result: lower rates of spending for welfare. We would hardly accept a similar explanation for gravity, claiming that rocks fall down because they are returning to the earth, but lead balls fall down because they are gray. An explanation either applies to a reasonably large number of cases, or it amounts to, They do it because that is the way they are. We need explanations that apply to more than one country.

One common approach to developing more general explanations is to hypothesize that those cultures that place a higher value on welfare will spend more on welfare. Unfortunately, this hypothesis tends to fall victim to a third logical error: the tautology trap. To measure the degree to which a country values welfare, we might well use the percentage of its annual GNP it spends on welfare. That measure sounds reasonable until one realizes that it is actually not a measure of cultural values but of how much is spent on welfare. It is surprising how often we find ourselves measuring values by behavior and then explaining that behavior with the values originally deduced from the behavior.[43] The only conclusion such an approach can possibly yield is that those countries which spend more on welfare will spend more on welfare. So stated, this seems like an easily avoidable error, but tautology is the single most common notation I find myself making on student papers.

Finally, there is culture as the residual. My classes always rebel against my arguments and defend the mystical concept of culture. They ask me to explain various phenomena without resorting to culture as a determinant. When they find something that I cannot explain, they triumphantly conclude that the only way to understand this particular phenomenon is by reference to culture. If we say culture causes everything we cannot otherwise explain, then a cultural explanation is little more than an admission of ignorance. Thus, as our understanding of Japan has grown, many cultural explanations have been replaced with explanations based on general comparative theories.[44]

Cultural generalizations tend to fall into one of the logical errors described above, but need not. General cultural explanations that cover many countries and that avoid all of the logical errors described here are quite possible. Developing such theories will not, however, be easy. The necessary data and theoretical constructs are not readily available. It may be easier to fall back on one or another of the logical errors that cultural explanations are prone to, so we need to inoculate our students and ourselves against the temptation.

If Not Culture, then Rationality?

The most popular alternatives to cultural theories are rational choice theories, and since I reject mystical cultural arguments, I may seem to be a rationalist. A rationalist believes that people are capable of correctly analyzing their situations and coming to accurate estimates of the optimal strategy for maximizing their self-interest. Harry Eckstein argues that "determining which of the two modes of theorizing and explaining—the 'cultural-ist' or the 'rationalist'—is likely to give the better results may be the single most important item now on the agenda of political science."[45] Given only these two choices, I would have to side with the culturalists. Cultural explanations need not be mystical, need not make logical errors, and can be as scientific and valid as any explanations.[46] On the other hand, the problems with the rational choice approach seem much less amenable to correction.

The basic problem with the rational choice approach is that it is poor psychology.[47] People do not routinely make sophisticated calculations of how best to maximize their self-interest. The fundamental assumptions of rational choice theory are simply wrong. Douglass North confirms that most economics do not really believe in the assumptions of rational choice: "Although I know of very few economists who really believe that the behavioral assumptions of economics accurately reflect human behavior, they do (mostly) believe that such assumptions are useful for building models of market behavior in economics and, though less useful, are still the best game in town for studying politics and the other social sciences."[48] Proponents of rational choice theory have offered several facile arguments to evade this problem, but the challenge is hard to ignore. Perhaps people act as if they were rational; but if so, why do they act that way? Perhaps false assumptions can produce accurate predictions, but on what grounds can we expect this result? If a theory based on false assumptions seems to work well, how do we make it better? What do we change if something goes wrong? How do we tell which set of wildly inappropriate assumptions would be better than another set of wildly inappropriate assumptions?[49]

Rational choice is also subject to many of the logical errors that afflict cultural theories. Rational choice is even more prone to the tautology problem than are cultural theories. The idea that people maximize their self-interest or utility is itself often a tight tautology.[50] Rational choice theorists often cannot answer a question about their own preferences because they have to wait and see how they act before they will know what they prefer. The only way to determine peoples' values is to see how they act. Whatever they do reveals their preferences, and those preferences explain what they do. This argument boils down to, People do what they do because that is what they do.

When people do things that seem stupid, are they really maximizing their self-interest? In rational choice theory, the only possible answer is yes; there can be no other explanation.[51] When we find ourselves saying something must be true, we are dealing with a matter of faith, not science. The fundamental trademark of science is not certainty but doubt. A scientist may build models and make deductions; but the key to science is experimentation, checking out the data. Scientists practice both induction, gathering lots of data and looking for patterns, and deduction, making assumptions and drawing conclusions based on those assumptions. Both are necessary. Pure induction can produce a list of facts that is little more than a list of trivia. Nevertheless, a systematically collected set of data usually yields some useful information. On the other hand, if the assumptions are invalid, pure deduction can be sterile and useless. Deduction produces hypotheses to be tested but can never replace data.

Rational choice theory assumes that people do not make mistakes. In a major defense of the rational choice approach, George Tsebelis argues: "If, with adequate information, an actor's choices appear to be suboptimal, it is because the observers perspective is incomplete."[52] He seems to be asserting that all action is both perfectly rational and the best possible choice available to the actor. Although he is remarkably consistent, even Tsebelis must resort to actors making mistakes to make sense of the world.[53] Let's face facts: people make mistakes all the time. Furthermore, attempts to approximate a rational decision are often window dressing. In a major alternative to rational choice theory, March and Olsen argue:

The primary source of the institutionalist challenge is empirical. Observers of processes of decision making regularly discern features that are hard to relate to an outcome-oriented conception of collective choice. Information is gathered, policy alternatives are defined, and cost-benefit analyses are pursued, but they seem more intended to reassure observers of the appropriateness of actions being taken than to influence the actions. Potential participants seem to care as much for the right to participate as for the fact of participation; participants recall features of the process more easily and vividly than they do its outcomes; heated argument leads to a decision without concern about its implementation; information relevant to a decision is requested but not considered; authority is demanded but not exercised.[54]

In other words, much of the activity that appears rational may well be rituals, performed after the decision has been made and intended to convince participants and observers that the right thing was done.

Tsebelis further argues that the "no mistake" assumption makes the rational choice approach more "scientific," stating: "Inconsistency between theory and reality is attributed to the inadequacy of the theory rather than to mistaken actors. As a result, the rational-choice approach lends itself to stricter empirical tests than most other theoretical approaches."[55] The assumption seems to be that, while rational decisions are predictable, mistakes are random. But this assumption is incorrect. We know quite a lot about how and when errors are made.

Participants in events tend to overestimate low probabilities and underestimate high ones, and attach higher probabilities to desirable outcomes than to others. They are likely to see history in a way that confirms prior beliefs or reflects favorably on themselves. They tend to attribute favorable outcomes to the intelligence of their actions and unfavorable outcomes to the actions of others, to exaggerate their own contributions to join products, to come to prefer those things that they can achieve. Because they are dedicated to the possibility of willful action, participants shape interpretations of history to emphasize the role of intention. Participants exaggerate the reliability not only of historical data but of history itself. They overestimate the likelihood of events that actually occur and underestimate the likelihood of events that do not occur but might easily have occurred, and exaggerate in hindsight their own foresight.[56]

Errors are predictable and are much more common than rational calculation and optimal solutions.

Mystical conceptions of culture, which posit a Japanese mind, are not helpful. Cultural theories seem to say that human beings are infinitely manipulable; they will believe anything they are told. We know better than that. Rational choice theories seem to say there is only one right answer, and everyone gets it right every time. We also know better than that. Most scholars, most of the time, take neither extreme view but tend to portray the other side in extreme terms. Culturalists say that rationalists cannot tell the difference between a person and a computer. Rationalists accuse culturalists of believing that people are stupid. I have portrayed both in extreme terms, because I think we can do better than either of these two approaches. It is tempting to say that the truth lies somewhere in between the two extremes, but half-and-half answers are even less useful than either of the original halves. We need a new approach: a more realistic view would see people as commonsense scientists.

People as Commonsense Scientists

People are "intuitive scientists who are gifted and generally successful, but whose attempts to understand, predict, and control events in the social sphere are seriously compromised by specific inferential shortcomings."[57] Commonsense scientists try to understand what is going on around them but have limited information and make predictable errors. They do not simply believe whatever their parents and teachers tell them. They learn from their own experience. On the other hand, they have neither the data nor the analytic capacity to figure out optimal solutions to difficult problems. They are quite capable of coming to conclusions that are both scientifically false and dysfunctional to society but that, nonetheless, persist for centuries. It is only common sense, for example, that the world is flat, as we do not see any curves. The kind of information necessary to understand that the world is a ball spinning in space has not, until recently, been available to the average person. In cases such as this, common sense will never lead to a scientifically correct conclusion.

Common sense comes from one's own experience. The information available from our own experience may be perfectly relevant to a particular time and place but is not a good source of information on how things work elsewhere. One's own experience is extremely limited, and thus the data a common-sense scientist uses to analyze the world is biased. I ran into one fascinating example of such biased data while visiting Kobe, Japan. Kobe is a simple city, laid out along the inland sea. Growing up there one learns that the mountains are to the north, the sea is to the south, and the trains all run east and west. Obviously, these generalizations apply only to Kobe, not to the whole world. But a friend who grew up there says he still gets slightly disoriented when he rides a train that runs north and south.

A somewhat more serious example concerns public opinion polls. Poll results are virtually guaranteed to violate our common sense, because no one talks to a random sample of people. Our common sense about what Americans are thinking about politics comes from the people we talk with about politics, and we tend to talk politics only with others who agree with us. Our data is biased. The great advantage of polls is not in the number of people surveyed but in the fact that the sample is unbiased. All other sources are biased to the extreme. We have access to excellent information on what our friends think, but our direct information on what the majority of Americans think is virtually worthless.[58]

As commonsense scientists, we can be fooled, but there are limits. We will not accept any theory that does not square with our own personal experience. We make mistakes, but we learn from them. If the relevant feedback is available, we will slowly but surely learn a very good, if not necessarily the optimal, answer. The best way to understand a nation made up of commonsense scientists is to study that country's recent history, its economic, political, and social structures, and to examine the early experiences of its people and the situations they face daily. If people are commonsense scientists, our best approach to social science research is a structural learning approach.

CHAPTER THREE

A Structural Learning Approach

If I am not a rationalist or a culturalist, what am I? I like to call myself a structuralist. I do not mean to imply, however, that I generally agree with others who call themselves structuralists. I especially wish to disassociate myself from the structural-functional school of thought.[1] I have in mind a specific definition of structure and a limited set of claims for the structural approach.

The factors that influence behavior fall into two categories. Situational factors determine the choices available to the actor; psychological factors determine which of the available options will be chosen. A structure may be defined as a relatively stable or repeated situation. A structural generalization predicts behavior from these stable or repetitive characteristics of the actor's environment. I make two claims for the structural approach. First, structural generalizations, when available, have several attractive characteristics. Second, the current state of the art in social sciences has overemphasized psychological approaches and underemphasized structural approaches. Thus, efforts to develop structural generalizations will have relatively high payoffs in the short run. In the long run, we will need better psychological theories to accompany better structural theories.

Structural Generalizations

Structural generalizations have several desirable characteristics, some of which have been claimed for rational choice theory.

47

George Tsebelis makes several claims for the rational choice approach that apply better to the structural learning approach. For example, he wisely abandons the defense of rational choice asserting that people act as if they were rational in favor of an argument based on the consequences of violating rationality. Thus he argues that "defending an axiomatic system (in this case, the combination of requirements that define rationality) usually entails demonstrating the plausibility of these requirements (axioms). However, a better argument can be developed by elucidating the undesirable consequences of violating such requirements; the more catastrophic these consequences, the more persuasive the argument."[2] It follows that only those violations of rationality that have noticeably negative consequences merit attention. We need to pay strict attention to the actual feedback from playing different strategies.

People often violate the requirements of rationality—for example, by having intransitive preferences (that is, if a person prefers *a* to *b* and *b* to *c*, logically he cannot prefer *c* to *a* but people often do.) We can also demonstrate that a person who consistently violates these requirements could be turned into a money pump: through a strategic series of bets, one could make an infinite amount of money from them. Which of these two facts is the more important? The fact that such a person *could* be turned into a money pump is interesting trivia. The number of people affected by a mathematical proof in an academic journal is too small to worry about. The proof only applies to people who are perfectly and consistently irrational, and such people do not exist.

What would happen if someone tried to use an actual "irrational person" as a money pump? The irrational person would not sit down and do a mathematical proof. He would learn from his mistakes. He would not continue to bet and lose money for long. He might rethink his preferences, making them transitive and thus becoming more rational. He might also decide that the person winning all his money is a wizard and deduce that one should never bet with wizards. His behavior would become more "rational," but there is no guarantee that his thinking would. In predicting behavior, we should pay no attention to potential consequences, only to actual consequences. We should pay particular attention to those consequences that cannot be ignored and should ignore those consequences that require sophisticated analysis or deductive logic to be recognized. We should not assume rationality, only that people learn.

The connection between structure and behavior is not rationality but learning.[3] A structural learning approach involves fewer and more plausible assumptions than does rational choice. One need only assume that the participants value the commodity being allocated and are capable of adjusting their behavior to avoid disaster and to seek success. People can be inconsistent, can at any given time have contradictory or intransitive preferences, and can make errors on a regular basis. If an action has serious consequences, either negative or positive, people will learn over time, through a process of trial and error.[4] The evidence does not support the assumptions of the rational choice approach. Observations that look like trial-and-error learning, however, are quite common. Abandoning the rationality assumptions yields gains in plausibility and predictive power.

Tsebelis makes a second argument about rational choice that also better suits the structural approach. "Because the only assumption regarding actors is their rationality, they lack any other characteristic or identity. They are interchangeable."[5] Interchangeability of actors is a useful characteristic in any generalization. If we need know little or nothing about the actors, the generalization will travel well, a characteristic particularly valued by people doing comparative studies. A structural generalization that works anywhere should work wherever an analogous situation occurs, because it does not depend on who is involved. If we know the game is baseball and that X is a third baseman, we can predict many things about X's behavior without any further information. Unfortunately, for rational choice theories to have the characteristic of interchangeability of actors one must assume that all people have the same tastes. Tsebelis acknowledges this point, though only in a footnote, but it is actually another way of sneaking an easily disprovable assumption into the model. Shall we assume that everyone prefers vanilla ice cream to chocolate? In a structural learning approach, actors are interchangeable because we need know very little about their preferences. All we need assume is that people are more likely to change their strategy in response to clear negative feedback than in response to clear positive feedback.

Both the focus on the consequences of the choices made and the claim of interchangeability of actors imply that the important factors are situational, not psychological. If our hypotheses are based on the argument that actors will avoid catastrophic consequences, we need know very little about the actors preferences, except that they avoid catastrophes. When consequences are catastrophic, the situation dominates. If actors are interchangeable, we need know only the situation and nothing about the preferences of the particular actors involved. In fact, game theory is an excellent tool for analyzing situations. Game theory is usually associated with rational choice but need not be. Rational choice is about preferences and can be dropped from the study of game theory with no significant loss. Game theory describes situations, the structure of opportunities, and incentives. It seeks to answer questions about what would maximize benefits in a given situation. The structural approach argues that, if the game is played repeatedly and if the players get strong, clear feedback, people will learn over time. Thus, game theory, with the untenable psychological assumptions of rational choice deleted, should be a basic technique for describing and analyzing structures.

A structure is a stable or repeated situation. One important type of repeated situation is a game. Games are often the essence of politics and provide the dynamic aspects of political structure. Politicians learn games, invent new strategies for winning them, and even adjust the rules periodically. Some political games are metagames that decide what the rules of other games will be. For example, the results of political games often change the rules of economic games. Politics often changes the parameters of economic games, for example, by raising or lowering interest rates. The game analogy is one of the most common ways of analyzing politics and with good reason. Politics is "an ecology of games."[6]

We may define a game as a repeated process with stable rules for allocating some valued good. Anyone who plays the game will learn the rules over time. Learning takes at least three forms: strategy adjustment, value adjustment, and exit. People with better strategies will tend to reap rewards, and people with worse strategies will tend to suffer. As Robert Axelrod puts it, "what works out well . . . is likely to be used again while what turns out poorly is likely to be discarded."[7] People learn from their own experiences, noting who wins and who loses and adopting the strategies of the winners. As people play the game, they also come to value the game itself, especially valuing the units in which the score is kept.

People changing preferences causes serious problems for the rational choice approach. If we predict behavior based on preferences, we must be able to assume that those preferences are stable. Unstable preferences destroy our predictive power. Unfortunately, the evidence indicates that values are affected by the environment and are, thus, subject to change.[8] Finally, if people find themselves in constant conflict with the values promoted by the game, they may exercise their exit option and stop playing. For example, a legislator who hates compromise will probably not like his job and is unlikely to seek renomination. Over time the game approaches equilibrium in an evolutionary process.[9] The equilibrium point can be predicted using a simple, relatively unsophisticated game theoretic analysis. The process will be trial-and-error learning at the individual level and evolutionary at the aggregate level. The probability of reaching and maintaining equilibrium will be affected by the consequences of being out of equilibrium.

The best documented structural generalizations concern budgeting. If we know X is involved in budgeting and works for a line agency, we can predict a great deal about X's behavior based on this information alone. Studies of budgeting in the United States, France, Great Britain, and Japan find several universal patterns of behavior that do not depend on culture.[10] If the country is rich and total revenue is known at the beginning of the process, budgeting will be incremental. The ministry in charge of budgeting will take the role of budget guardian, defending the budget against the free spenders. The line agencies will be advocates, asking for more than they can possibly hope to get. All requests will be cut, and the result will be very close to everyone getting the same percentage increase.

If revenues grow by 7 percent, agencies will ask for 10–15 percent and get about 7 percent.

We can easily predict the attitudes each actor will take. Everyone will hate the process and get cynical about it. Guardians and advocates will dislike each other, and the adjectives used to describe each will be similar around the world.[11] John Campbell tells a story about his experience researching in Japan. The bureaucrats he was interviewing would insist on explaining how the process ought to work according to the law, but after a while they would admit that what they really did was to see how much the total budget was going to grow, ask for that much more than their estimated need, and expect about the desired amount. They were certain that this was a uniquely Japanese failing and were embarrassed to admit that they did not budget rationally, as we do in the West. But, of course, this uniquely Japanese budgeting trait is also uniquely American, British, and French. Everyone is unique in exactly the same way, that is, much about budgeting is universal and does not depend on culture.

Of course, structure does not explain everything about budgeting. Nothing explains everything. First of all, there are variations on the theme. For example, some things about Japanese budgeting differ from American or British budgeting.[12] Second, there are exceptions to the rule, even in those areas that are best explained by structure. Incrementalism must sometimes give way to priorities and new programs. Most important, structure and situation do not always dominate behavior. Aaron Wildavsky found that rich countries with certain revenues budget incrementally; poor countries with certain revenues practice "revenue budgeting"; and poor countries with uncertain revenues do "repetitive budgeting." In each of these cases, much can be explained by knowing the basic structural parameters. However, no clear pattern emerges in rich countries with uncertain revenues. The situation leaves several options open, and Wildavsky adduces "cultural factors" to explain why a particular option is chosen.[13]

We are now on the verge of answering one of the greatest mysteries in social science: How can an approach like rational choice, which is based on false assumptions, produce hypotheses that work so well? The answer is: Rational choice may have the psychology wrong, but it describes situations quite well, and situations are much more important than we thought.

Culture as Evolving Repertoires

How does a commonsense scientist acquire culture? The most promising hypothesis is that he learns a set of standard operating procedures — socially defined repertoires of behavior. The idea of repertoires was originally proposed by historian Charles Tilly, who noticed that protest groups tended to follow a limited number of well-defined tactics that differed in time and place. Thus, "the idea of a repertoire implies that the standard forms are learned, limited in number and scope, slowly changing, and peculiarly adapted to their settings."[14] In some times and places, when someone suggests a protest, the question immediately arises: Who shall make the effigy? In other times and places, no one thinks of making an effigy, but everyone knows that we need to check with the local priest to find a time when the church is free, because the police are less likely to bother us in a church.

The concept of cultural repertoires fits neatly with the idea of the institutional state proposed by March and Olsen: "The institutional state is viewed as a political and moral order, and as a collection of long-lasting standard operating procedures reflecting values, principles, and beliefs that are shared by most of the population."[15] While I would argue that the idea that the institutional state actually reflects "values, principles, and beliefs that are shared by most of the population" is a politically convenient myth that social scientists should not swallow, the idea of "long-lasting standard operating procedures" meshes neatly with the idea of repertoires. The idea of culture as repertoires of behavior also fits neatly with trial-and-error learning at the individual level and evolutionary learning at the aggregate level.

On the one hand, repertoires are cultural. They consist of ritualistic behavior and symbolic action understood by the participants but not necessarily comprehensible to those from other times and places. Neither is a repertoire necessarily the single best solution to a problem. "Histories of organizational and institutional change are replete with stories of long stabilities of suboptimal strategies or technologies."[16] In the vocabulary of economic theory, "individuals make choices based on subjectively derived models that diverge among individuals, and the information the actors receive is so incomplete that in most cases these divergent models show no tendency to converge."[17] The QWERTY keyboard for typewriters, feet and inches, and pistons in internal combustion engines are all bad ideas. We know better solutions to each of these problems: demonstrably better keyboard layouts exist, the metric system has obvious advantages, and the wankel engine is clearly superior engineering. We do not adopt the best available answers because of the transition costs of changing over. Where we are depends on where we started. We do not reach the same solution, because did not start in the same place. Our choices are often "path dependent."[18] We can get caught in a "competency trap":[19] our engineers are capable of finding ways around the shortcomings of the piston engine, and so we do not spend the time and energy necessary to develop the wankel.

Repertoires are cultural, but they are neither irrational nor impervious to change. A repertoire is not the result of rational optimization, but it must work in some sense, or the participants will adjust the current repertoire or search for a new one. It is ritual but not meaningless ritual. It has instrumental as well as symbolic value. Culture as repertoire also makes it easy to understand how governments can influence culture. Tilly notes "the apparent success of authorities in channeling collective action from one form to another."[20] If the government decides to put policemen in the church, protestors stop meeting in the church. If the authorities do not respond to humble petitions, the people will try something else. When the situation changes, culture changes.

History as Changing Situations

A satisfactory concept of culture must be firmly anchored in history. Often the reason for different cultural behaviors lies in historical events. Seymour Martin Lipset (who, incidentally, claims to be on the cultural side of the culture-versus-structure debate) argues that "historical events establish values and predispositions, and these in turn affect later events."[21] His examples come from comparing the United States and Canada. It is hard to argue that Americans and Canadians are fundamentally different from each other. Mystical explanations are hard to defend in this case, but the cultural differences are quite real. Some differences can, for example, be traced to the fact that Canada stayed loyal to the English king, and many loyalist Americans moved north.

In studying history we can watch culture change. John Haley has analyzed the evolution of Japanese attitudes toward the law from 710 A.D. through the present.[22] He avoids both the cultural trap of assuming that some aspects of Japanese attitudes are constant throughout history and the rational trap of assuming that people understand and act on their self-interest. Although he does not address the issue of cultural change directly, the evolution of cultural repertoires is clear.

Recent research allows us to watch the evolution of the Japanese repertoire of protest and government repertoire for handling protest. Susan Pharr describes standard patterns of protest and response in Japan.[23] She argues that a typically Japanese response to conflict developed during the Tokugawa era (1600–1868). Prior to the Tokugawa era was a warring states period. People who study this era tend to think of the samurai ethic as "Stab your enemy in the back before he can stab you; poison him; hold his children hostage; do whatever is necessary to win."[24] The Tokugawa regime inaugurated a perod of peace and prosperity in which more honorable interpretations of the samurai ethic made more sense. The Tokugawa regime developed a way of dealing with social conflict: "Death, usually by decapitation or crucifixion, was the standard penalty imposed on protest leaders, even when the magistrate dealt positively with the protesters' demands and, in so doing, implied that there was some justice in their complaint."[25] And the system worked: even though there were many peasant protests during the 250 years of the Tokugawa era, "it was rare indeed for a locality to be visited by serious disorder more than once during the Tokugawa period or for a single village to produce leaders for more than one event."[26]

During the subsequent Meiji era (beginning in 1868), protesters were not put to death but were imprisoned, even if their complaint was justified. The great rice riots of 1918 forced the prime minister to resign and brought about both relief and reform. Protestors understood that they would have to pay a heavy price but that protest would bring results.[27] Throughout the prewar period, patterns of public protest interacted with government responses to protest; the repertoire was expanded and adjusted.[28] Because innovations were adjustments to the existing repertoire, many things remained the same. Repertoires of protest and response were not invented anew as a rational response to the specific situation but evolved in a process of trial and error. After World War II, the ability of the government to punish protestors was further limited by the reforms of the American Occupation. The standard government repertoire of response to protest had to be adjusted to fit the new parameters, but the pattern of response remained similar: "Your complaints are perfectly justified, but you have no right to complain."

Pharr argues that, "from this tradition, then, has come a pattern of social conflict management in which authorities seek to retain control of their prerogatives, avoid the creation of legitimate channels for resolving conflict, and marginalize protestors. Such a pattern allows authorities to grant concessions on their own terms and thus to control the pace of social change."[29] Pharr shows how this pattern of conflict management (not conflict resolution, because no attempt is made to resolve the conflict) has been applied to "status conflict," specifically intergenerational conflict, gender-based conflict, and Burakumin protest. Frank Upham applies a similar model to the cases of antipollution protests, the Burakumin, the women's movement, and industrial policy.[30] Thus, we have found a standard operating procedure of protest and response that typifies Japanese behavior over several hundred years. How should we deal with this finding?

This kind of long-lasting standard operating procedure is culture, but there are several apparent deductions that should

not be drawn from this finding. This repertoire is not a permanent characteristic of Japanese behavior: the technique was invented and had historical origins. It was not typical Japanese
behavior before the Tokugawa period. The patterns have evolved
over time in response to changing circumstances. Moreover,
this is only one of several techniques in the Japanese repertoire.
The Japanese sometimes use more direct suppression of conflict,
as evidenced by Prime Minister Kishi's response to the Security Treaty crisis in 1960 or the government's handling of the
protests in Narita Airport. I doubt that Japanese leaders really
like this type of response to protest. It is less a matter of values
than well-founded beliefs about what works well. If they could
suppress protest more directly, they probably would. Finally,
this is far from being a uniquely Japanese response to protest.
Indeed, it might well be called the Bismarck option: "Bismarck
sought to gratify the German public substantively, not proce-
durally."[31] The Japanese may use this repertoire more often than
most countries, but until we have actual comparative data from
other countries it is safer to admit our ignorance. We now know
one standard Japanese repertoire for protesting and handling
protest and should not claim to know much more than that.
It is neither the key to understanding the Japanese psyche nor
the secret to Japanese economic success, though it is useful information to have when analyzing or dealing with Japan.

Culture as Economic Structure

What is the best way to run a business? One strategy is to give
the customer good service to keep him coming back. An alternative strategy is to try to get the most money from any customer who comes through the door, by any means possible even
if it means never seeing him again. Most of my American students argue that the latter strategy is the sad but true fact about
the way the world works. When I asked this question in Japan,
100 percent of the students voted for the former strategy without hesitation. This fits our basic ideas about American businessmen being out for the quick buck and Japanese taking the
long view. It is a perfect example of a cultural difference. In
fact, neither strategy is absolutely valid. Which is the better

strategy depends on the situation, specifically on the probability of seeing the same customer again.[32]

If you were running a gas station located in a small town but on a major highway, the best strategy is to get as much as possible from every customer who pulls up to the pump, since the possibility of creating customer loyalty is nil. No matter what you do, you will never see this customer again. If you are on vacation and pull into such a station, you would be wise to doubt any suggestions they make about needed repairs.[33]

Now imagine running a gas station in the middle of a stable residential area in an urban area but not on a major highway. If you were to treat one customer badly, not only would you lose his business but the word would get out and you would lose the business of most of the neighborhood. The best way to make money in this situation is to give good service and create customer loyalty.

The Japanese believe in customer loyalty, and Americans tend to go for the quick buck. One reason for this difference is that America is much larger, with a more mobile population. Americans more often find themselves in situations in which the customer loyalty strategy is meaningless. Japanese live in a more stable and densely populated society. Japan is more like a gigantic small town, where everything everyone has ever done is common knowledge. Within America, the Japanese often seem more comfortable in the more stable and traditional areas, such as the South. Within Japan, people from Hokkaido, the closest thing to a frontier Japan, are reputed to be more like Americans.

What happens when an American is put into a situation in which the customer service strategy is clearly superior? I have used a gas station in a stable area of Boston, where I got what I considered excessive service, a feeling I often get in Japan. What happens when a Japanese is put into a situation in which the quick buck strategy makes more sense? I was shocked when I went into the duty-free shop in an American airport on my way to Japan. The employees were all Japanese, but they were also pushy, intimating that anyone who did not buy their full quota was stupid and pushing the most expensive brands. Upon reflection, I realized that they were in a situation in which it made no sense to try to build customer loyalty. One must consider not only a person's values but also their situation. In a situation in which one's cultural values make no sense, one learns.

Culture as Social Structure

Japanese students have a difficult time learning how to behave in the American classroom. They find it impossible to argue their case forcefully or even to ask questions of a professor. It often takes a year for them to adjust. But they do adjust: acting Japanese just does not work in the American classroom. When they return to Japan, they shock their professors with their aggressiveness. But they soon become Japanese again: acting American simply does not work in the Japanese classroom.

If people change behavior when they live in a foreign country, where is culture — inside people's heads or in the society? Much of what we mean by culture exists within social structures. Anyone living in a particular society would tend to act similarly after learning how things work. The most important part of socialization is not parents and teachers telling children how things are, but social structure. For example, Japanese children are not punished for hitting other children, and the teacher makes no effort to find out who started it.[34] No one takes the role of judge and jury. For Americans, it is only common sense that the teacher must intervene, make each child tell their side of the story, and decide who is right and who is wrong. The "trial" is a standard part of the American cultural repertoire, whether in a courtroom or not. It is not a familiar pattern in Japan.

The Japanese are often characterized as group oriented, while Americans are individualistic. The Japanese prefer security, whereas Americans value freedom. While these are excellent ways of describing the major differences between Japanese and American societies, these differences do not arise from differences in individual Japanese and Americans values. I have seen Japanese arrive and simply fall in love with the United States. They have been uncomfortable in Japan all their lives; they feel stifled by Japanese society, and when they begin to understand how American society works, they are set free for the first time in their lives. These individual Japanese have values that are more in tune with American social structure. On the other hand, I have seen many Americans fall in love with Japan. They have been uncomfortable in America all their lives. They prefer the discipline, warmth, and security of Japanese groups. Their values fit better with the Japanese social structure. I have also seen Japanese come to the United States and Americans go to Japan with great expectations, only to get immediately homesick. These people have values that fit their own societies. At the individual level, the values of individualism and freedom versus community and security vary more within than between countries. The big difference lies not in the values of the people but in the way the game is played, the kinds of activity rewarded in that society.

Most Japanese work in large organizations that provide great security, but the Japanese do not necessarily prefer security to individual autonomy. There are few jobs in Japan in which one has autonomy. Those few professions that provide both autonomy and security, notably law and medicine, are overwhelmingly popular, and the competition is intense. "Ask most Japanese *bengoshi* [lawyers] why they chose the legal profession as a career and invariably the answer will be that the practice of law enables one to have both security and autonomy."[35] More impressive is the number of Japanese who choose the high-autonomy, low-security career path of working for a small business. "Workers entering the labor market face a choice between comparatively stable employment as a life-long, blue-collar worker in a large firm or a short stint in a small firm followed by the high possibility of self-employment or managerial promotion."[36] Many Japanese prefer to be their own bosses. The differences between Japan and the United States have to do more with the options available than with the distribution of individual preferences.

In any organization, there is competition among individuals. The key competition in any Japanese organization is among individuals:

Despite the identification of individual bureaucrats with their bureau, private conversations that I have had with high officials suggest that the ultimate unit in conflict with other units is, as everywhere else, the single ambitious bureaucrat in rivalry with his immediate colleagues. The Finance Ministry official does not necessarily care much for the bureau that he defends at the expense of the unity of the whole; it is just that his quality as a loyal official will be judged by the success of his bureau.[37]

The basic competition is between individuals, just like everywhere else, but this competition is channeled by rewarding only team players. It is almost impossible to get ahead in a Japanese organization by stabbing someone else in the back. The Japanese social structure punishes mavericks and rewards team players. Japanese "groupism" does not come from some natural tendency at birth but from intensive training. The Japanese who tend toward individualism are forced into group structures.

> Those considered for top leadership positions are generally men with a surplus of energy, intelligence, and ambition, qualities they must learn to control and discipline in order to survive the long years of subordination to the organization, their superiors, and their office groups. For the average man this subordination may not be particularly difficult, but for talented and vital people it can be a struggle.[38]

Note that these potential leaders are forced to suppress their own individual tendencies; they do not cooperate because they are Japanese but because they have no choice. Note also that Japanese who have been in America long enough to learn that one can get ahead without promoting the success of one's current group often abandon their cultural background and backstab with glee.

Many of the Japanese behavior patterns that violate American common sense derive from the nature of groups in Japan. There is a socially sanctioned common process of group formation in Japan, part of the standard repertoire of Japanese culture. The Japanese who get together to perform a task go to great lengths and spend an inordinate amount of time producing the proper group dynamics. The effort is necessary precisely because it is not natural. "The cultural factor here is not that such conflict-within-cooperation relationships emerge 'naturally' in Japan. In fact, they are difficult to establish and require sanctions to prevent defections. It is rather the assumption that this sort of mechanism is preferable to either free competition or bureaucratic command if each participant is to maximize his benefits."[39] Although Campbell suggests that the Japanese believe this mechanism is "preferable," I would argue that they believe it is "effective." They may or may not like it, but their experience has taught them that it works.

Culture as the Current Wisdom

It has often been argued that structures are themselves reflections of cultural values. Structures are institutionalized choices from the past, which reflect cultural values.[40] But this is only partially true. Cultural values are only one of many influences on the decisions that are institutionalized in social structures. Social structures were not created at some particular point in time. They have evolved, and continue to evolve, in complex processes. Social structures are not the result of a unitary set of values but the result of conflict, compromise, and evolution.

One mechanism for the evolution of social practices is the competition among organizations such as businesses. When one management style seems to work better than others, it is copied and becomes enshrined as the best practice. It is taught in business schools and enforced by banks and creditors. One of the most instructive of these cases concerns Mazda.[41] Mazda was not a typical Japanese company. It was run from the top by an individualistic and autocratic boss. It was run American-style, and it did quite well. It even had the American characteristics of risk-taking and innovation. When General Motors and other large companies decided that developing the Wankel rotary engine was too big a project for a single company to take on, Mazda, one of Japan's smallest companies, took it on and made a success of it. In this case, Mazda acted more like our image of an American company and General Motors acted more like our image of a Japanese company.

Unfortunately, in the middle of this venture oil prices skyrocketed, and the high-performance, gas-guzzling rotary engine turned into a losing proposition. Mazda was in trouble.

Under some pressure from the government, Mazda's bank stepped in to guarantee the company's debts and restructure its management. By the time the bank finished restructuring, Mazda fit our stereotypes of Japanese management very closely. Mazda is now run on the Japanese management system, not because its people are Japanese and have different values from us but because the established wisdom in Japan is that companies run by individual entrepreneurs do not make money. They believe their postwar experience proves this to be the case. When Chrysler had similar problems, the American answer was to ask John Wayne, in the form of Lee Iaccoca, to ride into town and clean up the mess.

The Japanese believe that collective leadership is better, and Americans believe that individual entrepreneurship is better. This is an excellent example of what cultural values are. It is not that all Japanese, or a majority of Japanese, or even the average Japanese believe in collective leadership. In fact, smaller companies, prewar companies, and perhaps many other types of Japanese companies are not run on the Japanese management system.[42] It is rather that the current wisdom in business circles is that collective leadership is better. The current wisdom, or "ideas in good standing," varies both among countries and over time.[43] For example, the idea of democracy has gone in and out of fashion throughout modern history, often depending on the results of the last war.[44]

The Japanese management system exists primarily in two places. In the American literature on management, Japanese management practices are not necessarily what Japanese managers do, but those things that some Japanese managers do that are considered worthy of emulation.[45] The primary purpose of this literature is not to describe Japan but to reform America. In the minds of Japan's financial establishment, the Japanese management system is the current wisdom of the management community about what works best. The Japanese distinguish between the *tatemae* (the principle of the thing) and the *honne* (the actual facts of the matter). The current wisdom is the *tatemae*. It is invoked whenever companies get into trouble. "The scandalous magazines continually harp on the demerits of 'one-man' presidents; and whenever a company goes bankrupt or suffers a great loss, the serious journals almost invariably diagnose autocracy."[46]

Institutions also codify the values of the past by rewarding those who fit the values of the system. Security conscious people rise to the top of security based organizations, and those people tend to make decisions based on a preference for security centered strategies. Creative people rise to the top of entrepreneurial organizations, and they tend to make policy based on a preference for risk-taking strategies. People who win under a given system will tend to support that system. The system thus has a strong tendency to reproduce itself, independent of the values held by the majority of its members. Only the leaders of the organization need have values that fit the structure of the organization to keep those values intact.

The relation between structures and values is complex. I do not claim to have solved this puzzle. But the idea that structure reflects an unchanging core of cultural values is a dead end. The idea of both structure and culture evolving in response to the environment and as a product of conflict and compromise is much more accurate historically and a more fruitful avenue of research.

Culture as Equally Valid Responses to Universal Problems

If you have a problem with a friend, what is the best way to handle the problem: to bring it all out in the open and clear the air, or to wait in silence and hope the problem will go away? The former is the standard American answer, the latter, the standard Japanese answer. Americans are among the most talkative people in the world, explaining everything at lengths that the Japanese and Europeans often consider excessive. The Japanese coming to America are often told that, while in Japan they can be understood without words, in America they must say it out loud to be understood. The Japanese often pride themselves on "stomach talk" (haragei), that is, nonverbal communication.

Nonverbal communication sounds like magic. Maybe the

Japanese really are different. I was relieved to learn that one common plot on Japanese "home drama" (TV soap operas) involves two members of a family on a collision course that neither knows about. Mother assumes that everyone else in the family understands that young Ichiro (a common boy's name) will be going to college. Meanwhile, Ichiro assumes that everyone understands that he will be joining the family business. Everyone assumes that there is no need to say any of these things out loud. When the disagreement finally comes out everyone is embarrassed and upset. The resulting argument takes months to resolve, because the two parties directly concerned do not talk. Third parties must mediate.

There is an old Japanese joke about a town drunk who claims to be spiritually enlightened. A group at the bar decides to find out if he is really enlightened by inviting a famous Zen monk in to test him. The monk meets the drunk and initiates the conversation with a gesture. No words are spoken. The priest begins by making a large sweeping gesture with both arms. The drunk responds with a tiny gesture, using two fingers, and the conversation continues without words. The drunk steps out, and the group anxiously asks the Zen monk if the drunk passed the test. The monk assures them that the drunk is indeed enlightened. "I started with a gesture meaning that all the world is one. He responded perfectly with a gesture that means that everything is contained in microcosm in the smallest object." The priest goes on to interpret each gesture in terms of Buddhist theology. The monk leaves and the drunk staggers back into the bar. He was surprised to find that the monk is such a good guy. The drunk says, "He began with a gesture meaning that sake comes in very large barrels. I responded by pointing out that we drink it in tiny cups."

The Japanese often understand what others are thinking without asking. They are much better at nonverbal communication than Americans are, for two reasons. First, they practice a lot. In America, there is little need. If a misunderstanding arises, the counterargument, "You never said a word," wins hands down. No one can be expected to be understood unless they say something. The second reason for the greater ability at nonverbal communication is that the Japanese share more context than Americans do. The number of things that require explanation are fewer.

There is less variety in Japanese lives than in American lives.[47] First, though subcultures do exist, the range of subcultures is nothing like that found in the United States. The dominant culture is much more dominant. In many ways, everyone in Japan is a salaryman, even the farmers. The Japanese first arriving in the United States often ask seemingly silly questions like, "Do Americans spank their children?" or "Do Americans take showers in the morning or baths in the evening?" In Japan there is an answer to these kinds of questions that will predict the behavior of over 90 percent of the Japanese population. Japanese do take baths in the evening and wash their faces in the morning. No such statement can be made about Americans. In fact, I doubt we could find a statement about American behavior that is true for 75 percent of Americans that is not also true for 75 percent of the human race.

Second, basic life patterns are the same for virtually all Japanese. (This uniformity of life patterns is a postwar phenomenon.) Thomas Rohlen paints a picture of the people working in a Japanese bank associating almost exclusively with other members of the bank, and mostly of the same age. The bank career is so predictable that, to fit in, one must get married and have (precisely two) children at about the same age as one's colleagues.[48] If you have three children, an explanation is called for. If you have no children or more than three, others will have a hard time understanding your behavior, no matter how much you explain. My Japanese students are always amazed by the variety in the basic life stories of adult Americans.

In Japan, all students take entrance exams for high school and for college at the same age. Some, called *rōnin* (masterless samurai), may stay out a year or two to study for the college exams, putting them a bit behind, but basically all college freshmen are the same age. Almost everyone gets a job right after graduation and stays with the company for the rest of their lives. There are exceptions, and those people must explain themselves continuously (just like foreigners), but for most people most of the time, there is not much to explain. We had a Japanese student at the University of Alabama who was simply delightful, full of life, but somehow not quite like any other Japanese anyone had ever met. The explanation turned out to be simple. She was an Olympic athlete and had never had to go through "exam hell." She had missed this quintessential Japanese experience and was, therefore, a bit different. Even the Japanese agreed that she was different in a very pleasant way.

Returning to the question asked at the beginning of this section on the best way to deal with a disagreement among close friends, I would answer that Americans seem to bring things out in the open, fight over them, and say things that cannot be taken back and leave permanent scars, when, had they waited a week, the whole problem might have disappeared. Americans fight unnecessarily. On the other hand, the Japanese wait and hope that problems will disappear. They let small problems fester until they are big problems and cause irreversible damage to relationships.

The American system of discussion is probably an effective way of dealing with about 75 percent of all interpersonal problems, causing serious negative consequences only about a quarter of the time. On the other hand, the Japanese system can also handle about 75 percent of the problems, failing only in the 25 percent where the American system is necessary. In half of the cases, either system works reasonably well. If one system becomes accepted, the feedback will always be positive: it will work most of the time. Once it becomes a society's accepted way of doing things, there will be resistance to change, and people will tend to continue doing it. This *is* a matter of teaching values. Whichever value a society teaches, each generation's own testing of reality will confirm much of the wisdom of their parents and teachers. It is a self-fulfilling prophecy.

Some cultural differences persist and are immune to changing circumstances, because they are equally valid responses to universal problems. If people experiment first with what they have learned from their parents and teachers and abandon only those things they find unworkable, these cultural differences will persist over the centuries. Whichever value is tested first will prove to work most of the time. However cultural values first emerge, over time they become the standard wisdom, taught

by parents and tested and confirmed by each succeeding generation. The value has become institutionalized, a part of the
social structure.

Culture as Modes of Expression

The aspects of culture discussed thus far are of interest primarily to social scientists. Those aspects of culture that are of the
greatest practical importance are quite different. The most convincing evidence of a national culture is the fact that one's common sense does not work in other countries. We tend to assume
that a difference in common sense is a difference in basic values. But it is often the case that the basic values are exactly
the same, though the means of expressing them are different.
The substance is the same; only the form differs.

To start with a simple example, when a Japanese wants someone to "come here," he will gesture with his arm outstretched
but his palm down. The American gesture has the palm up.
To an American, the Japanese gesture often communicates "go
away," a miscommunication that can lead to serious consequences, even though it could hardly be a reflection of basic
value differences. Which is the "right" side of the road to drive
on? It makes no difference as long as everyone drives on the
same side of the road. The "right" way to signal "come here"
is the way that others will understand.

The Japanese palm-down gesture makes no sense to Americans but it does seem a bit sissy, especially to a macho young
Hoosier. When I was first in Japan, I decided that I would ignore this cultural artifact. (This happened before my umbrella
experience.) After all, how could anyone mistake the meaning
of the American gesture? It is just common sense. I found myself on the street trying to hail a cab. I raised my hand, as one
might do in New York. The Japanese taxi drivers stared at me
but did not stop. I tried two hands. This produced more stares
and a few laughs but no stops. After the fifth or sixth cab passed
me by, I decided to adjust to Japanese culture. I gingerly put
my hand out palm down and waved. I felt embarrassed but I
had two cabs competing for my business in a matter of seconds.

Another early experience taught me how to say no in Japanese. I needed a duplicate key made. I had the basic grammar down and had looked up all the relevant vocabulary but did not at that time speak much Japanese. My plan was to enter a likely looking shop and ask, "Do you make keys here?" If the answer were yes, I would simply hand them my key. If the answer were no, I would ask, "Where do they make keys?" I knew quite well that I had no chance of understanding the answer to this question, but I figured I would get some idea of the general direction I should head; surely they would point in some direction. I would go that direction and ask again until I had the shop where keys are made bracketed. As soon as people started pointing in the opposite direction, I would know that the correct shop was somewhere in between the two stores where I had asked the question. Armed with my Japanese dictionary, my plan, and the whole afternoon in which to accomplish this simple task, I set out to get a key made.

My plan went awry immediately. I entered a likely looking shop and asked, "Do you make keys here?" The answer was, "Saaa. . . ." I quickly looked up this word in my dictionary and found that "saa" means "well." I understood what the man said but had no idea what he meant. I knew the words for both "yes" and "no" but he refused to use either one of them! The shopkeepers were very polite. They tried their best to explain, but their explanations were too long and complicated and did not contain either the word for *yes* or the word for *no*. As I latter discovered, the Japanese do not like to give clear negative answers. If the answer is yes, they will say so. If the answer is no, they will avoid answering the question directly. Any Japanese will understand that a question avoided is a question answered in the negative. Americans, however, get confused. One might argue that this is a difference in values. Americans like clarity, and the Japanese like to avoid conflict by never saying no directly. Perhaps; but do Americans really like clarity, or is it simply that, in America, no one understands us unless we express ourselves clearly.

To finish my key-making story, I had one happy experience but an unhappy ending. I went into one store and asked, "Do you make keys here?" The young clerk seemed to understand my situation precisely. She spoke slowly and clearly, using a phrase right out of my textbook: "No, we do not make keys here." I thanked her and left immediately, happy that I had understood every word and unwilling to venture into the unknown by asking, "Where do they make keys?" In the end, however, I got no key made that day, despite spending four or five hours trying. Somehow I had the image of a key-making store as a small shop. I wandered all around outside of a large department store, where keys are actually made, but I never entered. (I discovered the place to make keys later by accident, when I was shopping for something else in the department store.)

Another significant source of misunderstandings is the difference in the way the Japanese and Americans find out about new acquaintances. In this case the Japanese are more direct: they simply ask. An American who wants to know another's name will not ask, "What is your name?" despite the prominence of this phrase in English conversation textbooks in Japan. An American will say something like, "Hi. My name is Steve Reed." The other person will almost automatically respond with his name. If he does not, it is a clear indication that he does not wish to continue the conversation. If he does wish to keep the ball rolling, he will tell you not only his name but something else about himself, perhaps where he works. The conversation can last a whole evening without one direct question being asked.[49]

I have often met Japanese in social situations and spent the whole evening talking with them. At the end of the evening I know nothing about them, but they know everything about me. I go home thinking, "You know, Japanese really are sneaky. He grilled me about the details of my life but told me nothing about himself." My Japanese friend probably went home thinking, "You know, Americans really are self-centered. I expressed great interest in his life and he talked about himself all evening. But he never expressed the slightest interest in my life." Stereotypes are reinforced, but the real difference is simply in the way one requests personal information from others. It is a difference in form, not substance. When dealing with Japanese students, I force myself to ask questions. I am uncomfortable, feeling that I am being pushy and impolite, but they respond with glee to the professor's expression of interest in them.

One can attribute this particular cultural difference to basic values: Americans consider direct questions a violation of privacy, whereas the Japanese consider it impolite to volunteer information about themselves without a clear expression of interest from their conversation partner. It is always easy to explain things after the fact. If you had to deduce from general cultural values which people ask direct questions and which pursue an indirect strategy, you would come to the mistaken conclusion that the Americans use the direct approach and Japanese the indirect.

In general, I advise people going to Japan to read all the books on Japanese culture and the Japanese mind, and to memorize each example but not to buy the general theory. If you go to Japan expecting the Japanese to be exactly like us, you will be surprised by many things. It is precisely those things that surprise Americans that are put into American books on Japanese culture. On the other hand, if you go to Japan thinking you have learned the key to Japanese values, your deductions about Japanese behavior will be mistaken about half the time. Using a cultural theory will work as well as flipping a coin. You are much better off memorizing these cultural differences, one at a time, than trying to discover a secret key to unlock underlying differences.

For people who deal with the Japanese, this contextual detail is much more important than any discussion of core values. These are the kinds of differences that produce misunderstanding and miscommunication, precisely because they are differences in the way people communicate. If you wish to communicate effectively with people from other cultures, you need a lot more than a dictionary. You need to know what the Japanese would say in a particular situation, not how to say in Japanese what an American would say in that situation.[50] It would be nice if all this detailed contextual knowledge could be encapsulated in some key phrase, one magic concept that explained all Japanese behavior, but what we need is detailed contextual knowledge that can only be learned through a long period of experience and memorization. It is simply a matter of details.[51]

Much of culture is simple custom. The Japanese from different parts of the country love to discuss the New Year's customs of their hometowns. Such discussions are less common among Americans, but most are fascinated by the varieties of Christmas customs around the world. Each of these customs comes with a rationale. There is no scientific explanation; it is only custom.[52] But understanding customs is extremely important for anyone wanting to live in the country or to get along with the people.

What Persists and What Does Not

One of my basic arguments is that culture changes at a generational pace; it is not eternal. Yet some aspects of culture seem to last forever. Part of this is an intellectual trick: we search for things that do not change and create vague generalizations that cover all of history. Nonetheless, some aspects of culture do persist over long periods of time.[53] It is easy to assume that this persistence can only be explained by long-standing core cultural values. There are, however, other sources of social inertia that need to be explored. Change is often stymied by the myriad interrelated details in the current situation. Some of these details may reflect past values, but many are negatively valued, and most were hardly conscious choices at all. A great deal of social inertia comes from details that were decided incidentally, even accidentally.[54]

Some aspects of culture persist over long periods of time. First, there are ideas for which no feedback is available. If each new generation has no way of testing an idea, there will be no reason to reject that idea. Religion is the prime example. If you were told as a child that thunder is caused by Zeus throwing thunderbolts, you are unlikely to change your mind and decide that it is really a group of giants bowling. Culture-specific forms of communication and response, like those discussed above, also tend to persist over time. These customs are learned from one's parents and teachers and are borne out in practice. Self-fulfilling prophecies should also persist indefinitely.

One might argue that anything that has persisted for centuries has proved difficult to change and that it is therefore part of the cultural core. Let me propose the counterhypothesis, that any cultural trait that has persisted for centuries is probably peripheral. It has persisted only because there has been no reason to change it. The classic explanation of why Japan has the longest reign of a single imperial family is that the Japanese emperor played no practical role in government. Japan could thus move from a warring-states period to a feudal period to a modern nation without ever having to overthrow the monarchy. The emperor never got in the way and was a useful symbol of continuity. The imperial symbol persisted precisely because it was only a symbol. An analogous American example is the electoral college. Technically, the American president is not elected by direct popular vote but by a college of electors. As long as this remains an obscure technicality the electoral college will endure. There will be no reason to change it. If, however, the electoral college ever takes on importance by overruling the popularity majority vote, it will not last until the next presidential election.[55]

What Culture Can Explain and What It Cannot

At the end of a lecture or talk on culture, people often forget that I am arguing about *why* people are *different* and somehow come to the conclusion that I am arguing that all people are the same. My most basic argument is that mystical explanations, in which no mechanism for transmission of culture is specified, are nonsense. I also argue against any conception of culture as a set of core values that persist over the centuries. A serious case for such a concept can be made from the functionalist assumption that all aspects of a society must fit together in a smoothly functioning organic whole. However, I am not a functionalist, and I worry that the search for an eternal core is a futile quest analogous to the search for a panacea in medicine.

Socialization is the dominant hypothesis for explaining national differences: the Japanese are different from Americans because Japanese parents and teachers teach their children ideas that are different from those taught by American parents and teachers. While not denying a major role to socialization, I argue that one important aspect of culture is common sense, what people learn from their own experiences. The commonsense hypothesis may be states thus: the Japanese are different from Americans because they grow up in a different environment and their experiences lead them to different conclusions about the way the world works. The best way of understanding peoples' most basic ideas is to understand the environment in which they grew up. I am not trying to explain basic values. I am trying to explain basic concepts about the way the world works: the best way to run a business, the best way to deal with disagreements among friends, legal problems with neighbors, and the police.

I also argue that culture is not of a piece. I reject the idea that all aspects of culture are a reflection of core values or even that all aspects of culture are related to each other. I find no reason to believe that gesturing with the palm down is related to the use of umbrellas or the tendency to ask direct questions of acquaintances, and none of these is related to either the samurai ethic or Confucianism. I further suggest that we would be better off breaking down the concept of culture into more manageable concepts. As a beginning, I have suggested culture as a set of ideas about how the world works, as values, and as modes of expression. In any case, culture as the Japanese way of thinking is a useless concept.

Students often think that I am arguing that culture is unimportant. In one sense they are correct: culture is unlikely to be an important explanation for things of concern to comparative social scientists. For example, I find no reason to think that Japan's phenomenal economic growth was caused by Japanese culture. To the degree that culture is conceived of as eternal, a constant, it cannot explain change. It makes no sense to say that Japan started growing rapidly in 1960 because they are Confucian. If Confucianism is a cause, Japan should have started growing when it became Confucian, not centuries later.[56] More important, if culture changes in response to the environment, it is more likely to be changed by growth than to cause growth. For example, do the Japanese work hard? They did not in the Meiji era. "Japanese workers of this era were neither keen on taking orders nor enthusiastically committed to their jobs, and persuading them to submit to the discipline of factory labor was no easy task; it was far from accomplished by the turn of the century."[57] It is far more likely that Japanese workers started to work hard when working hard paid off in terms of income and advancement, that is, after economic growth had begun in the 1960s.

Direct cultural causation of major economic, political, or social changes is improbable. On the other hand, major economic, political, and social changes are certainly shaped by contemporary culture. All change occurs from where one is to begin with, and the starting point can make significant differences in the end point. For example, I do use culture as a commonsense explanation to help explain Japanese economic growth. It is currently common sense to Japanese managers that one cannot rest on one's laurels, one must continually improve the product to stay competitive. Why? Not because of the samurai ethic. Their postwar experience is one of rapid change, in which anyone who fails to keep up with the newest trends is soon out of business. As Ronald Dore puts it,

> The whole experience of rapid growth over the last twenty years, and the rapidity of Japan's transformation in recent decades, shifting her from the status of a backward country claiming special dispensation to protect its infant industries from competition to that of a leading industrial power, has diffused throughout the nation — among trade unionists and production workers as well as among managers and bureaucrats — a *general* conception of the inevitability and even desirability of continuous structural adjustment, of positive adjustment as a positive good.[58]

The Japanese economy has changed and growth is now slower, but older ideas persist and have significant effects on current behavior. The managers who never experienced the high-growth era will act differently when they take over their companies.

In this context, culture may be thought of as the terrain over which change must occur. If we have two perfect ball bearings on frictionless planes, one near Phoenix and one near Los Angeles, and we give each exactly the same push to the west, they will not wind up in the same place. Ten miles west of Phoenix is not ten miles west of Los Angeles. In the social sciences, we are seldom allowed to work with analogs of perfect ball bearings and frictionless planes. Social science is more like dealing with two misshapen boulders, one in Phoenix and one in LA. The same force applied to both produces different results because the starting point is different, because the boulders are of different shapes, and finally because the boulder that started in Phoenix is headed toward mountains, while the boulder that started in Los Angeles is soon underwater. Why did the boulders move? Because of the force applied. The explanations for change are universal and do not depend on context. But you cannot explain what happened to the boulders without talking about the terrain on which the change occurred. Economic growth is caused by the same factors everywhere. But a poor, over-populated, peasant society may follow a different path of economic growth from that of an urbanized, merchant society.

Finally, I argue that culture as modes of communication is extremely important, if not to economists and political scientists, then to visitors and anyone who needs to deal with the Japanese. One should not mistake differences in modes of communication for differences in basic values, but one must know culture in order to communicate effectively. Unfortunately, culture as a mode of communication is a matter of contextual detail. There is no alternative to simple memorization and practice.

CHAPTER FOUR

Making Common Sense of Permanent Employment

*W*hen *I begin explaining* Japanese permanent employment to my classes, at least one student objects if people can't be fired they won't work. They'll all sit around doing nothing and collect a paycheck for loafing all day. That's the U.S. post office!! And everyone knows that the post office is a horrible way of doing business. At the University of Alabama I developed a technique of letting the student rave as long as he wished and then extending the argument as much as possible, getting the whole class to agree that permanent employment cannot possibly work. Once everyone is convinced that the Japanese system is hopelessly inefficient, I conclude that we have now proven beyond a shadow of a doubt that there is not a single Toyota in the parking lot. After about five seconds, the class agrees that the parking lot is full of Toyotas, Hondas, and other Japanese cars; therefore, the Japanese system must work reasonably well. Only after this shock treatment are they ready to listen. If your theory proves that there are no Toyotas in the parking lot, and your eyes see lots of Toyotas in the parking lot, something is wrong with your theory.[1] When theory and facts do not match, the theory must be changed.

The idea of permanent employment violates some of the most basic premises of American common sense. We "know" that permanent employment cannot work. Nevertheless, over the years I have developed explanations that make American common sense of permanent employment. In the context of Japanese labor and management, permanent employment makes perfect American common sense. The first step in explaining permanent employment to American students is to shock them out of their preconceived notions by "proving" that there are no Toyotas in the parking lot. The second step is to discuss what permanent employment really is.

What Is Permanent Employment?

To understand what permanent employment is, it is useful to ask what it is not. Japanese workers do not have contractual rights to permanent employment. Contracts in Japan are notoriously brief. In one bank, "new members sign a statement, called a 'contract' (keiyaku), that documents only two things: recognition of the person as a member of the bank, and his pledge to follow the rules of the organization."[2] Permanent employment is not a widely understood concept among the Japanese. The term permanent employment comes from sociological studies of Japan, not from labor-management negotiations or common parlance. In Japan, "there is no widely used term among workers that refers to their rights in this area. If one asks workers whether they have shūshin koyō, a relatively new term popularized through the translation of James Abegglen's book into Japanese . . . they will often register confusion as to what you mean."[3] Permanent employment is not an absolute commitment by management never to fire anyone, nor by workers never to quit. Everyone understands that economic realities may necessitate reduction of the work force and that people do quit. In fact, companies with thirty to ninety-nine employees tend to fire, for disciplinary reasons, about 1 percent of their workers every year. Companies with over five hundred employees fire only one of every three or four hundred workers per year.[4] These numbers are small but not zero.

Yet, even though it is neither a legal contract nor an absolute guarantee, permanent employment is real; it makes a difference in how Japanese management treats its work force. Permanent employment does imply that incompetence "is no excuse for firing someone. People unable to do their jobs are normally transferred to posts of little responsibility."[5] Keeping some incompetents on the payroll is the cost of maintaining morale among all workers. Permanent employment also discourages long-term layoffs and dismissals. In the 1975 oil shock recession, Japanese companies were forced to reduce their labor forces, but "cutbacks of regular males employed in manufacturing occurred almost entirely without dismissals and indefinite layoffs took much longer than in the United States or Germany."[6] Actual layoffs were rare, and those that did occur were negotiated with the labor unions.[7] In 1975, the combined number of "departures at the employer's initiative," that is, firings and formal voluntary early retirements, increased to 3 percent for companies with thirty to nine-nine employees and to more than 1 percent for companies with over five hundred employees.[8]

Permanent employment can best be understood by keeping two basic concepts in mind: first, the firm is something akin to a family, where all employees are "members" of the firm; second, a psychological contract exists between the employer and employee, which implies a mutual loyalty. The bank studied by Thomas Rohlen "is not regarded in everyday thought as primarily a legal entity or a complex money-making machine, but more as a community of people organized to secure their common livelihood." The company is an economic organization, but it is more than that. "The member agrees to work wholeheartedly for the organization, and the bank agrees to serve the needs of the member. Money and labor are central, but they must be understood as resulting from a more general commitment."[9] Note that "money and labor are central": the basic economic facts remain universal. Japanese workers work for money, not out of loyalty to their firm nor commitment to national goals. As long as they are paid and treated reasonably well, they will remain loyal. If they are paid or treated badly, their loyalty will shrink until it is eventually exhausted. The Japanese may initially be more loyal to their firm than Americans, but the dynamics of increasing or decreasing loyalty are the same. Permanent employment originated in part from an attempt to fool workers into thinking of the company as an idealized family. In the end, workers forced management to live up to many of its promises.

Members of the Japanese firm are locked together by psychological, organizational, and economic ties. They belong to a community. They have no choice but to deal with each other and, therefore, must get along as best they can, just like families. Divorce (in the form of quitting or firing) does happen but is an unhappy last resort. For the most part, it is better to stick it out (*gamman suru*) and make the best of it. The Japanese assume that, barring unforeseen circumstances, one will work for one's company for life. "Irregular departures are embarrassing and unhappy affairs similar in atmosphere to marital divorce."[10] Permanent employment is the norm for most of the people they know. Exceptions do occur, but they are embarrassing and require explanation.

Like other cultural artifacts, people tend to believe in permanent employment even when the evidence before them disproves the myth.

> Many workers went further than merely accepting "lifetime employment" as a principle. They even suggested that Marumaru, like most other companies, was practicing it. . . . They knew, of course, that women and temporary workers were not employed for life, that young men were leaving in droves, that union members who opposed the management too violently would be got rid of, and that employees at the small factory were being strongly encouraged to do so. They were able, however, to reconcile the actual insecurity of employment at Marumaru with the thesis that "lifetime employment" existed by reference to imagined conditions in the West. I was told by employees of all grades, including managers who had made trips to America, that any worker in the West who made even a tiny mistake would immediately lose his job.[11]

These workers' depiction makes permanent employment in Japan seem more than it really is and makes the United States seem more different from Japan than it really is. The image erases the complex of exceptions in reality and fits permanent employment more neatly into the theory of how things ought to be (*tatemae*). This simple image is then compared to an even more simplified (and often mistaken) image of America. The realities are different, but much closer together than the images would suggest.

The Japanese assume that they will work for the company for the rest of their working lives and that the company will take care of them. This assumption amounts to a psychological contract that the worker will neither be fired nor quit. Usual estimates of how many Japanese workers really have permanent employment range from 20 to 35 percent. Those are estimates of the percentage of workers for whom the promise of permanent employment can be kept: permanent workers at firms large enough to be safe from bankruptcy. Understood as a psychological contract, however, virtually all Japanese workers have permanent employment. It is also more difficult to fire temporary workers and women than one would expect. One reason so many small businesses in Japan go bankrupt is that they have trouble firing people. Instead, they declare bankruptcy and reorganize with a smaller work force. Historically, there is evidence of "long-term employment commitment on the part of these small-scale paternalistic employers. That is, such employers sought to abide by traditional ideology despite the objectively high risk of failure."[12] In Japan, permanent employment is the norm. All companies strive to achieve that norm, so that they will be considered good companies, which consequently attract good employees and are trusted by the banks.

We may think that the Japanese really are different from Americans because Americans do not need psychological contracts; we rely on written contracts. This may be one of those rare instances in which our common sense about Americans is wrong. In fact, this is the same error made by the Japanese workers quoted above: believing the theory more than the evidence will support. We are taught that the United States is a contract society, that, in the end, one can depend only on a written contract; it follows that Americans depend only on the written word. In fact, we too depend on psychological contracts and revert to the courts only as a last resort. The recent rash of mergers and takeovers has violated the psychological contracts of many workers. "Shaken by mergers and cutbacks, today's managers fend for themselves, placing their trust not in corporations but in their own capabilities."[13] That sounds like what Americans always thought they were doing, and it has been true to some extent; but as the economic environment has become less predictable, American employees have changed the ways they think about their companies, moving reality closer to the image of individual initiative that we have been taught to believe. People in their sixties confirm that companies in the United States used to be more like Japanese companies are today.

Who Benefits from Permanent Employment?

Permanent employment is a psychological contract in which management agrees never to fire a worker if the worker agrees never to quit. Would an American manager offer this deal to a worker? My American students certainly would not. American managers would not give up the right to fire their workers, because they need the threat of dismissal to maintain discipline and provide incentives to work. Would an American worker accept the deal? Few of my American students thought they would give up the right to quit just to gain the security of never being fired. In fact, many American workers interpret permanent employment as akin to slavery.

Neither American management nor American workers would accept the permanent employment deal. This makes the Japanese seem even more inscrutable. In a similar situation, not only would an American manager act differently, but American workers would act differently as well. This is a clear cultural difference. But much of this perceived difference is due to an incomplete understanding of the situation in Japan. Once the situation is understood, Japanese behavior makes American common sense and, in a similar situation, Americans would act much like the Japanese.

Who benefits from permanent employment? The American view is that no one benefits; both management and labor would be foolish to accept the permanent employment deal. Which viewpoint is correct, scientifically valid? The answer is quite simple: it depends on the balance of the supply of labor and the demand for labor. When there is a labor surplus and there are not enough jobs, the right to quit is not the right to find a new job but the right to be unemployed. The right to fire, however, is the right to get rid of troublemakers and to choose the cheapest and most docile among the many other applicants. When there is a labor surplus, the market is good for management and, therefore, the permanent employment deal favors workers.

When there is a labor shortage, the right to fire is the right to get rid of one worker and search for a qualified replacement. One may well have to pay the replacement more. When there are a lot of jobs, the right to quit is the right to leave one job and choose the most interesting and best paying of the many alternative jobs available. In a labor shortage, the market favors labor and, therefore, the permanent employment deal favors management.

If you want to know what a person will say about permanent employment, ask if they are American or Japanese. If you want to know how a person will respond to an offer of permanent employment, you would probably be better off asking about the current labor market in their country. In the past ten years, my American students have almost unanimously said they would reject any offer of permanent employment. However, in bad economic years, when jobs are scarce, seniors, after a moment's reflection, begin to see some merit in the idea.[14] As we shall see below, Japanese attitudes toward permanent employment are also influenced by the current market situation.

Debunking Mystical Cultural Explanations

American companies hire workers to be productive and fire the incompetent in order to remain competitive. American economic theory teaches that ownership (management?) *is* the firm and that workers are just one input. Production can be based on either labor-intensive techniques (using lots of workers) or capital-intensive techniques (using lots of machines). Workers, far from being "members" of the firm, are equivalent to machines, employed as long as they are more useful than machines and fired when machines become more efficient.[15]

Permanent employment fits most of our stereotypes about Japanese culture: groupism, paternalism, and so on. However, there are several reasons to reject simplistic cultural explanations. First, the practice of permanent employment has changed over time. It was not prominent in the early industrialization stage, became more widespread after World War I, and was institutionalized only after World War II. If Japanese culture comes from the ancient past, the samurai tradition, why did permanent employment start only after World War I? A constant cannot be used to explain change. Second, permanent employment is not a uniquely Japanese phenomenon. Other peoples at other times in other places have come to similar solutions to their problems. Moreover, this is another of those cases in which comparing Japan to the United States makes Japan look unique when, in fact, it is the United States that is the strange country. Third, the evidence suggests that Japanese workers think a lot like American workers and that Japanese managers express the same values as American managers. The differences are less in the psychology of the participants than in the structure of the firm. Fourth, the practice of permanent employment is institutionalized primarily for permanent, male workers in large firms. In other areas of the Japanese economy, quitting and firing are common. Finally, in each of these cases, we can explain the deviations from the norm of permanent employment by reference to the particular economic situation the workers and managers find themselves in.

Cultural Change

Permanent employment was not a characteristic of Japanese management in the Meiji period. In the early 1900s, managers complained that Japanese workers had too little loyalty and were overly motivated by the love of money. "Especially in times of prosperity when workers are in short supply, there are many who, on the basis of a trifling difference in wages, will readily switch to another factory . . . or who constantly move from one large factory to another."[16]

Permanent employment was encouraged by employers after World War I, when a labor shortage made it profitable for workers to change jobs in search of higher wages. Employers drew on traditions of paternalism, telling workers that the company was like a family. However, the "language and ideology of paternalism did not impress working men of this era for good reason: the early glorification of beautiful customs of paternal care had little grounding in actual practice."[17] In fact, workers "had been taught by managers how different they were from respectable folk. . . . They entered work through separate gates, they ate separately, they used separate toilets, and on leaving work at day's end, they were subjected to a body check."[18] It is difficult to convince workers that they are members of the family while performing a body search to look for stolen company property. The workers were seldom fooled and never for long. Abraham Lincoln's famous aphorism, "You can fool some of the people all of the time, all of the people some of the time, but you cannot fool all of the people all of the time," applies to the Japanese as well as Americans.

After World War II, unions demanded and got promises of job security. In effect, they demanded that employers live up to the promises they had made in the prewar period. Soon thereafter, the economy began to boom, and there was no need to fire anyone. Nevertheless, whenever a recession occurred, management called for reform of the practice of permanent employment. "With great fanfare, the Japan Federation of Employers' Federations announced during the recession of 1965 its support for the establishment of an American-style layoff system — though it was to be adapted to Japanese conditions. Unions and workers, however, showed strong resistance and were pretty much able to hold the line."[19] In times of labor surplus, management suggests changing the permanent employment deal. Once the deal was struck, however, it proved difficult to change. At any given time, either management or labor wants to change permanent employment, and the other party wants to keep it. Which party will favor and which oppose the deal is a function of current labor market conditions. The battle generally ends in a stalemate, leaving the system of permanent employment little changed. Maintaining the status quo is always easier than changing it. Permanent employment has been institutionalized in Japan.

Robert Cole observes that "the postwar expansion of permanent employment occurred at a time when the Japanese people, at least on the surface, were rejecting traditional values as having carried the seeds of a disastrous war. Hence, at this time, the spread of permanent employment should be seen primarily as a response to market conditions."[20] Certainly, permanent employment was not sold as a return to traditional Japanese values, because at the time no one supported the values that had led Japan into World War II.

The practice of permanent employment fits Japanese cultural patterns neatly but cannot be explained as a direct reflection of cultural values. Permanent employment also made good economic sense at the time. When it did not make good economic sense, the Japanese did not practice permanent employment. Permanent employment is not a reflection of shared cultural values. Instead, it is a compromise among conflicting values rationalized with arguments rendered familiar by long usage in Japanese culture.

Is Permanent Employment Uniquely Japanese?

Permanent employment is probably the best example of mistakenly drawing from comparisons of Japan and the United States the conclusion that Japan is a strange country. Workers are seldom fired in Japan and often fired in the United States. In fact, with regard to permanent employment, Japan is similar to most countries of Western Europe.

Several different pieces of evidence lead to this conclusion. One survey asked blue-collar workers aged twenty-five and under in many countries how many times they had changed jobs. Figure 4-1 shows the percentages of respondents who had never changed jobs. Japan is the highest and the United States the lowest, but Japan is only 8.4 percentage points higher than Germany, while the United States is 13.9 percentage points lower than Great Britain. If Great Britain were left out, the position of United States would be even more extreme. In any case, we need create no special category for Japan. If Japan has permanent employment, then France and Germany have semipermanent employment or pseudopermanent employment, or something similar. The United States must then have ephemeral employment, probably inspired by the deep American appreciation of the fleeting cherry blossom.

The socialist Mitterand government in France enacted laws

Figure 4-1: Percentage of Youths Never Having Changed Jobs

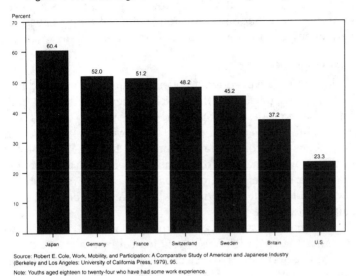

Source: Robert E. Cole, Work, Mobility, and Participation: A Comparative Study of American and Japanese Industry
(Berkeley and Los Angeles: University of California Press, 1979), 95.

Note: Youths aged eighteen to twenty-four who have had some work experience.

making it more difficult to fire workers, and the results have
tended to make French firms look more like Japanese firms.
"There has been an unanticipated congruence between reforms
that employers rejected initially (the Auroux Laws) and the development of more favorable attitudes towards the firm and
the economic conditions for its success on the part of workers
(and the French more generally). Today, business leaders admit privately that there has been considerable change, which
they owe, in large part, to the Left."[21] Economic conditions have
also played a role in the development of enterprise unionism
and permanent employment in France: "In part, the new tendencies toward enterprise-based unionism reflect continuing
high levels of unemployment. In a context in which the only
plausible alternative to employment at one's current job is unemployment, workers are likely to see themselves as lifetime
employees of the same firm and to develop greater loyalty to
their enterprise."[22] We would be unlikely to explain the development of permanent employment and enterprise unionism by

referring to French culture. The fact that similar circumstances produced similar results in two countries also makes it easier to argue that economic conditions were the major causes of permanent employment in both France and Japan.

Labor's Perspective

Japanese workers often do want to quit. Rohlen found that "only the rare person in [the bank] has never considered quitting. Most consider it seriously enough to speak to others about it. Few, however, actually quit."[23] Moreover, the Japanese and Americans quit for similar reasons (see table 4-1). Contrary to the popular image of the Japanese worker, more Japanese than Americans left their jobs because of a desire for "mobility and self-fulfillment." Individual values cannot be deduced from cultural premises.

If so many Japanese workers think about quitting, why do so few actually do it? The psychological commitment to the firm can be overcome. Divorce does happen. But there are other, more concrete, reasons not to quit. Because of cultural condi-

TABLE 4-1.   *Reasons Detroit and Yokohama Workers Give for Leaving Work (percent)*

Reason	Detroit	Yokohama
Financial	25.2	16.4
Job security	5.6	9.4
Job dissatisfaction	20.2	15.5
Mobility/self-fulfillment	16.1	20.7
Involuntary dismissal	21.4	15.3
Personal non-job-related	9.0	19.0
Other	2.5	3.7
Summary		
Push away from old job	61.1	62.1
Pull toward new job	26.0	25.1
Combination of push and pull	3.4	0.7
Ambiguous	4.2	5.5
Non-job-related	5.3	6.5

Source: Robert E. Cole, *Work, Mobility, and Participation* (Berkeley and Los Angeles: University of California Press, 1979), 88–89.

tions, the Japanese take longer to be affected by the concrete reasons. "The elasticity of the relationship is expressed by the fact that in the event the exchange becomes 'unbalanced' (that is, unsatisfactory to one party), it may continue for a considerable length of time utilizing the reserve of forbearance, good will, and trust implied in the original commitment."[24] That they hang on longer does not mean, however, that they ignore the real world. They may quit a bad job later than an American would, but they quit for exactly the same reasons. Japanese management is less likely to fire a troublesome worker, but the reasons to want to fire a worker are exactly the same. Culture has an effect, but the concrete reasons for permanent employment are more significant.

First of all, in a society in which staying with one firm for life is the norm, anyone who quits is viewed with suspicion. In the United States, employers look askance at a vita that shows too many job changes. The employer wonders whether this applicant can hold down a job. In Japan, employers have doubts if there is even one job change on the vita.

The second and more important reason Japanese workers quit less often than they may wish is that pay and promotion in a Japanese company depends heavily on the number of years with the firm, a system called *nenkō joretsu* (seniority pay) by sociologists. Because it is assumed that everyone will join a company upon completion of the last year of formal schooling, be that middle school, high school, or college, and will stay with that company for life, it makes sense to pay people by seniority. Younger employees are underpaid but know they will make it up later in their careers, when they will be overpaid. People who do change jobs lose their seniority and must begin again at the bottom, or close to it. They will spend more time being underpaid and less time being overpaid. Actually, the "longer a mid-career entrant stayed the closer his treatment approximated that of school entrants his age; but mid-career entrants would probably reach a given standard rank between two to ten years after coeval school entrants, and then only if they were able."[25]

Japanese workers accept the permanent employment deal because to quit is to lose money and promotions. To change jobs in Japan is expensive. In a similar situation, what would American employees do? They might not act exactly like the Japanese, but they would not have any difficulty understanding why Japanese workers do not quit whenever they feel like it. We noted above that French workers tend to stay with one company longer when jobs are scarce. In fact, Americans do not quit whenever they feel like it either. The business and employment climate, rather than cultural values, determine the likelihood of workers changing their jobs.

Japanese workers do sometimes quit. "Reliable statistics show that for firms with 1,000–4,999 employees, only one-third of male blue collar recruits are new graduates and that the remainder have some work experience at other firms."[26] Permanent employment is the ideal (*tatemae*), but the fact (*honne*) is that people do sometimes quit and are sometimes fired. More important, the groups that do have higher turnover are easily comprehensible to American common sense.

First, during the high-growth era, one category of employee was quite mobile: middle school and high school graduates (that is, people who did not go on to college). Companies lavished attention on these people, but demand exceeded supply, so jobs were easy to find and people changed jobs. "So high is the leaving rate among less educated young workers that it can be said to be normal for a man to leave his first employer, and abnormal for him to stay with his first employer for any length of time."[27] Demand and supply has an effect in Japan, as elsewhere. The workers acted rationally, but management was more influenced by the ideal of permanent employment. "Instead of behaving as our imaginary 'rational' employer might, and encourage 'mid-career entrants,' Marumaru spent tens of millions of yen trying to recruit high school leavers who were known to be unlikely to stay, and completely ignored its mid-career entrants."[28]

.The most important group of workers with high turnover rates is that in small firms. Japan has often been characterized as a dual economy, a few large companies surrounded by myriad *kogaisha* (child companies) often subcontracting for the larger companies. "In Japanese manufacturing, 46.5 per cent of workers have jobs in establishments with fewer than 50 workers, slightly more than in Italy (44.4 per cent) and much more than in the United States (15.2 per cent) and the United Kingdom (15.9 per cent). The other Western European countries fall between 16 and 50 per cent but are closer on average to Italy and Japan."[29] Japan is very different from America, but Japan is nearer the mean than is the United States.

Small businesses are simply unable to provide a guarantee of permanent employment. "There are market situations which do not allow traditional practices and ideology to operate. Such is the case in many small-scale firms where . . . the high rates of interfirm mobility are based on high bankruptcy rates, low wages, unstable product demand, and a shortage of capital funds."[30] Small firms try to provide job security, and the attempt is one reason for the large number of bankruptcies. The result is that "young workers in small plants move from one firm to another so frequently that the annual separation rates are more than 30 per cent. Although these rates drop to about 15 per cent when these workers are in their thirties and forties, they are still about 10 percentage points higher than the rate of Japanese workers in large enterprises."[31]

Until recently, we pictured workers in these small firms as poor, underpaid, and exploited. However, current research indicates that there are good reasons to work for a small firm. "Generally it has been argued that they [workers in firms with under thirty employees] are the source of the recorded lower wages and poorer working conditions, but careful investigation reveals that there is a career pattern that often leads to the ownership of a small business."[32] As a small business grows, it spins off other small businesses. "If expansion continues, the point will be reached when the entrepreneur, in turn, agrees to set up one of his employees as a subcontractor. Why would he want to do this? It is difficult to keep skilled workers satisfied in this industry [machine shops] after they have six to eight years of experience."[33] Small businesses cannot keep workers by promising them security, so they offer a chance for future self-employment. Blue-collar workers have a choice:

> Workers entering the labor market face a choice between comparatively stable employment as a life-long, blue-collar worker

in a large firm or a short stint in a small firm followed by the high possibility of self-employment or managerial promotion. The lifetime wage payments made to such workers are more or less equal. Only small-firm employees who fail to open a firm or be promoted suffer substantial wage losses as compared with blue-collar workers in large firms.[34]

Some workers choose the security of the large firm, others prefer to take their chances, hoping to own their own businesses.

Our general picture of the Japanese is that they prefer security. However, though Japanese society may be constructed to provide security, that is not necessarily what most Japanese want. Some sacrifice security to become their own bosses. In fact, although small businesses often go bankrupt, new businesses open faster than the old ones close. "This degree of entrepreneurial vitality comes as a surprise, given the stereotype of the Japanese as a cautious, risk-averse people who prefer the security of stable well-defined relationships."[35] Japanese society may be dominated by security-oriented people, but the Japanese are not necessarily security-oriented. The Japanese who prefer some risk must either adjust or find peripheral niches in society.

Management's Perspective

American managers tend to believe that if workers cannot be fired, they will not work at all. Japanese managers say the same about Japanese workers. "In every factory section heads and supervisors told the same stories: if you ordered an extra hour of overtime, or ticked off a worker for being careless, or even raised your voice to make yourself heard over the noise of the machines, the next thing you knew was that someone had resigned, and someone else was taking time off to look for a job."[36] In fact, Japanese employers admire the American system, though they do not understand it.

Admiration for the American system, one understood to permit dismissal on a wide variety of grounds, is sometimes voiced by leaders who also mention a belief that lethargy, bred by an over-dependence on the company, could never develop in America. They quickly add that there is no reasonable hope of adopting American procedures in the bank, for morale would be destroyed, and the company union would become active.[37]

Japanese management admires the American system, where employers are free to fire at will, and American management admires the Japanese system, where people work hard because they are loyal to the firm. Neither understands the other system and might not like it so much after taking a closer look. After operating under the other system for a while, they would find much that was perfectly familiar. Again, the differences in American and Japanese theories (*tatemae*) are much greater than the differences in practice (*honne*).

Japanese managers often argue that it is a generational problem. The younger generation has lost the loyalty and work ethic of the previous generation. Unfortunately for this theory, the facts indicate that the earlier generation was also lazy and lacked loyalty. "The argument that young people left because they belonged to a corrupt modern generation was vitiated . . . by the fact that the supervisors and managers who were so ready to berate young people for their 'selfish' modern attitudes, had themselves changed companies in their youth for what had presumably been selfish reasons."[38] Actually, it is a well-documented fact that the younger generation has been going to hell in a handbasket since at least 500 B.C. Moreover, it has been doing so in every country of the world. Of course, the only evidence for this theory is the testimony of the older generation, but the older generation always seems absolutely certain of their "facts."

Japanese managers would like to be able to fire people, but they do not. Why not? An American manager in the same situation would surely fire someone. Isn't that a cultural difference? Yes, it is, but there are also real differences in the situation faced by American and Japanese managers. There are at least three reasons why a Japanese manager might not fire an incompetent worker: it would ruin morale, the union would object, and the courts might intervene.

The dismissal of workers violates the Japanese psychological contract between managers and workers and thus ruins morale. The recent rash of mergers and firings has ruined morale in many American companies. When regular layoffs occur, workers begin to think about changing jobs. They stop focusing on the job in front of them and start focusing on their future. If your company may not be part of their future, they will pay less attention to your company. That is just common sense anywhere in the world. In Japan, a company that fires people is a bad company to work for. Firing a worker for incompetence is not worth the price in lost efficiency in the rest of your work force.

Americans generally think that Japanese unions are weak because they have little influence on the shop floor. Japanese unions are usually docile, but they do strike when the company fires people. Strikes in Japan are most often caused by disputes over layoffs. Management is reluctant to risk activating the union and jeopardizing their generally cooperative relations with labor.

If management fails to consult the unions, the unions can take the matter to court. "There are numerous precedents recognizing employer obligations to consult with the union when discharge or layoffs are contemplated."[39] Americans tend to think of Japanese courts as weak and ineffective, but again, we have found an important exception to the rule. "The courts, however, influenced by the practice of lifetime permanent employment, have developed extensive legal rules which restrict management rights to some extent. The fundamental principle here is that it is an abuse of the employer's right to discharge his employees if the discharge is not based on 'just cause.'"[40] Management's reluctance to fire a troublemaker and risk losing a consequent court battle is certainly understandable from an American point of view.

Again, the final argument in support of the situation, and not something inside their heads, as the determinant of Japanese management practices comes from Japanese organizations that do not practice permanent employment. In an organization completely staffed by Japanese but organized more like an American company, how will people act—like the Japanese or like Americans? I know of no organizations in Japan that fire people as often as American companies do; but public corporations follow other American-style management practices. In public corporations, top management is recruited from outside, from people retiring from government ministries, and lower level employees can never rise to the top. It is a two-class system, much like American companies. Will the Japanese be loyal to their firm even when permanently assigned to the lower class in that firm? Kenneth Skinner has done an excellent study of a Japanese public corporation.[41] He found serious conflict between the top-level management who came from the ministry and those below them, including adversarial relations with the union, more individual responsibility for specific tasks, and less group responsibility, high-handed one-man leadership styles, and attempts by small groups of conspirators to force the removal of superiors. This constellation is not unfamiliar to observers of American business relations.

The Evolution of Permanent Employment

The prewar labor market was not characterized by job security, let alone permanent employment.[42] The standard procedure at large firms in the 1920s "was a hiring system in which a minority of inexperienced young boys regularly entered a firm each year as a favored group expected to become future workshop leaders and career employees, while managers drew the majority of factory laborers from a pool of mobile, often unemployed adult wage earners."[43] Managers, however, found it useful to try to persuade workers that the company was like a family. "The invoking of traditional symbols was an attempt to render it familiar — to map the behavior that employees were now expected to display."[44] The idea that Japan had a unique family system for managing the firm was also useful in avoiding government intervention into the entrepreneur's affairs. "Businessmen directed their praise of paternalism (onjoshugi) as much at the government as at the workers. Bureaucrats lobbying in favor of a factory law beginning in the 1890s provoked leading capitalists and company managers to extol time and again the beauty of old Japanese customs of loyalty and benevolence."[45] Thus, Japanese businessmen used techniques found in their cultural repertoire to keep their workers docile and to prevent government intervention.

The war changed things. All prewar practices were placed in doubt, because they may have contributed to the disastrous defeat. Moreover, Americans were trying to democratize Japanese structures. The American Occupation democratized labor relations, giving labor the right to strike and generally promoting unions. First and foremost, these newly empowered unions demanded job security. In the early postwar period, Japan was desperately poor. People without jobs starved. Workers expected to be treated like members of the firm, as white-collar workers were. In essence, they demanded that management's prewar promises be kept. Their demands were not passive pleas for management benevolence; they were backed up by strikes, violence, and factories run without management. There were even assassinations and derailed trains.[46] Management, at first uncertain how to proceed under the Occupation, struck back with union-busting tactics, especially after 1949. The labor history of Japan before the early 1960s belies any belief in the innate cooperativeness and nonviolence of the Japanese.

All this conflict resulted a renegotiation of the basic labor-management deal.[47] Labor won the first round, management the second. At the end of the second round, management stood victorious, but the renegotiated agreement favored labor more than the prewar system had. In order to win, management had to make some promises. They essentially promised that the red purge and massive layoffs were one-time events, never to be repeated. They probably had no intention of keeping that promise, but labor unions have been extremely sensitive to layoffs ever since, and they have proved quite capable of forcing management to live up to its bargain.

A major piece of the renegotiated deal was permanent employment. Neither management nor labor got what they wanted: it was a compromise forged in conflict. Both sides remained determined to continue negotiating until they got what they really wanted, but the third round of negotiations was called off due to economic growth. When the economy started to grow rapidly in the 1960s, the stakes were lowered, because there was enough money to go around. The growth also confirmed the wisdom of the deal. Permanent employment "worked": it was the practice in effect when growth began. No need to fix things that are not broken. During the high-growth era, management and labor would complain about the postwar deal, but there were no serious challenges. The level of conflict dropped as people's incomes doubled every five years.

During the years of high growth, the permanent employment arrangement was institutionalized. Workers became members of the firm. Kazuo Koike has shown that white-collar workers in France, Germany, Great Britain, the United States, and Japan all have similar wage profiles and act more or less as if they have permanent employment. Japanese blue-collar workers are treated much differently from blue-collar workers in the other industrial democracies: they are treated like white-collar workers. He calls this phenomenon "white-collarization."[48] Gordon finds that Japanese workers in the early postwar period demanded to be treated as members of the firm. Koike finds that Japanese blue-collar workers in the 1970s have become white-collarized. By the 1970s, the early postwar labor-management deal had been institutionalized.

This basic story of a postwar reopening of negotiations on the labor-management deal, high levels of conflict, some movement toward labor preferences, and the institutionalization of whatever was in effect when growth began in the 1960s characterizes Western European countries as well as Japan.[49] Moreover, another basic finding of this research on Europe also fits the Japanese case: that when economic hard times resurfaced in the 1980s, negotiations picked up right where they had left off. The precise demands of labor and management differed from country to country, depending on the history of labor-management relations and the economic situation at the time, but there is no reason to make a special case of Japan. The Japanese story is similar to the stories of the other industrial democracies that were devastated by World War II.

Why Permanent Employment Works

By this time, the idea of permanent employment should make solid common sense in two important respects. First, the reasons why neither Japanese nor American workers and managers quit and fire at will should be clear. In both countries it depends on the circumstances. Second, it should also be clear that permanent employment developed as a compromise solution to the conflict between management and labor. It was not the preferred solution of either management or labor or a direct reflection of deeply held Japanese values. But the most basic American commonsense argument is that permanent employment should not work. They may have good reasons for practicing permanent employment, but it should ruin their economy. Why doesn't permanent employment produce lazy workers and hamstrung management? Why does permanent employment work?

Let us begin with the toughest question: If workers cannot be fired, what is their incentive to work hard? Imagine yourself in a permanent employment situation. You can plan on working at this company for the next twenty or thirty years. You could quit, but it would cost you. You are basically stuck. What would you do? You would probably complain a lot about how unfair the world is, but you are doing that anyway. How do you get ahead in this situation? How do you make more money? The first answer is that your fate is tied to the company. If the company fails, you fail. The only way you can make money is for the company to make money. The boss is right when he tells you that the company is like a family and everyone must work together, that the key to success is teamwork. To hurt the company will hurt you, to help the company grow may help you personally. There is no good reason not to work.

But neither is there any particular reason to work hard. Your effort will not make a great difference in company profits, and any profits you make for the company will be shared with everyone. To motivate people to work hard requires carrots and sticks. American companies need big carrots and big sticks to keep other companies from stealing their best workers and to rid themselves of their worst workers. But in a more stable situation, small carrots and small sticks prove wonderfully effective.

When workers are tied together in a company for long periods of time, gestures of preference for one employee over another become significant.

> The immobile employees linked to the company by loyalty, self-interest, and the difficulty of leaving, were destined to live and work together for twenty or thirty years. Among these men bound to get on with each other, competition was relentless. . . . Since promotion, at least in some parts of the company, was so nearly

automatic, the gains and losses in the struggle were apparently slight. But so thoroughly did everyone know the biographical details of everyone else and so nice were the calculations of precedence, that to reach a grade a month or two ahead of one's contemporaries might be accounted a considerable success.[50]

Tenured professors should be familiar with this phenomenon. Tenure makes it difficult to change jobs, so that dissatisfaction with salary decisions amounting to less than fifty dollars a year can grow into a major political issue. Unfortunately, professors do not have to cooperate with the rest of the department to do their jobs, so one does not find familylike atmospheres, even on the surface of most academic departments.

In the Japanese permanent employment situation, workers cannot get ahead by stabbing others in the back. First of all, backstabbing hurts the company. More important, backstabbing can be kept a secret for only so long. In America and Japan, workers prosper when they are deemed valuable to their companies. But, under its permanent employment system, Japan's management has more time in which to judge a worker's competence. The characteristics that win in the short run are not the same as those that win in the long run. In Japan, "all men are judged according to their performance over a long period of time. Qualities of personal charm and persuasiveness are of little significance in this situation, compared to the value of persistent, dependable, and careful work."[51] The American phenomenon of the twenty-five-year-old self-made millionaire is unheard-of in Japan. These whiz kids would never make it in Japan. Japanese workers are expected to prove themselves over a decade or longer, doing many different kinds of jobs for the company.

Japanese individuals compete fiercely with their coworkers, but they cannot get ahead by backstabbing. How much energy is wasted in American companies in backstabbing battles over who should get credit for a success and who should be blamed for a failure? How many good ideas are squelched by office politics? There is much less waste in a Japanese company than in an American company, not because the Japanese are nicer, not because the Japanese are less competitive, but because the structure of competition inside the Japanese firm forces people to cooperate. Permanent employment and other policies of the Japanese firm mean that the only way for an individual to get ahead is to help the firm make money. The invisible hand of market forces leads people to work for the good of the company.

Japanese firms are like families. People are locked together for most of their lives, and they learn to get along. Most of the time, personal relations inside the firm are reasonably satisfying. The social dynamics of an American firm are quite different.

> High turnover and the expectation of job changing have a profound impact on any organization: diluting human relations, emphasizing the impersonal, sharpening differences of background and interest, sponsoring individual competition, and generally fostering alienation from the organization and its goals. In America today these qualities are widely viewed as the results of large-scale organization, but studies of Japanese organizations remind us that all of these undesirable qualities derive also from the pattern and degree of individual mobility in large organizations, and this is a quality that undoubtedly varies with culture and time. Like it or not, we must recognize that our cherished sense of individual independence from organizations greatly accounts for the unpleasantness of social relations we experience within them.[52]

Japanese companies are like small towns. Everyone knows everything about everyone else. Reputation is everything. It can be stifling, but it can also be comfortable. In either case, it focuses everyone's attention on the goals of the company.

In order to make permanent employment work properly, to create the familylike atmosphere, a firm must have a specialized product line. Japanese companies tend to be specialized and to have homogeneous work forces. The focus is on the product and producing a better product at a lower price, not on financial balance sheets. "[One] consequence of functional specialization is to lessen the emphasis on financial management within the firm. The language of management in a diversified company necessarily has to be finance, for its separate divisions have nothing in common besides their contribution to the company financial results."[53] If competition forces companies to produce a better product at a lower price, Adam Smith's invisible hand turns individual greed into economic benefits for all. When competition is focused not on product improvement but on financial management, what does the invisible hand produce?

The key reason that permanent employment works is that it makes the company the unit of competition. "Competition is between companies, rather than individuals."[54] "The sense of corporate unity does give an edge to the zeal with which the men of Toyota do battle with the men of Nissan which is rare in other countries. (Toyota could no more think of employing an ex-Nissan executive, for instance, than the wartime British army would have inducted a captured German officer into its ranks.)"[55] Individuals do compete, but in so doing they contribute to the health of the company. In Japan, companies compete to make a better product at a lower price. In America, individuals compete to make more money any way they can. Which more clearly embodies Adam Smith's concept of the free market?

Why Japan Practices Permanent Employment

It is not at all uncommon for the final conclusion of a scientific study to be that the question as originally asked was stupid. Although it is hard not to be disappointed with this finding, it is in fact among the most useful possible conclusions. One may not be able to answer the question asked, but one has learned more about how the world works. The question, Why does Japan have permanent employment? turns out to be an ill-conceived question. Permanent employment is not a uniquely Japanese phenomenon, and employment is not really permanent in Japan. There is a continuum among industrial democracies from high job security systems to high-turnover systems.

We could ask why Japan has the highest level of job security, but it is better to ask what explains the level of turnover among industrial democracies. It is not a question about Japan. It is a question about job security. It is best asked as a comparative question: Why do some countries have higher job security than others? At this point the reader should remember my basic bias. I am a dedicated comparativist, and the fact that I have concluded that the problem of Japanese permanent employment is a comparative question should come as no surprise. Basically, I have concluded that my original biases were correct. I hope I have presented enough evidence to convince you, but you should certainly look at the evidence yourself and not take my word for it.

If we knew why industrial democracies develop high or low job security systems, we would then know why Japan has high job security. The proper way to answer that question is a comparative study. I have done no comparative study, so I can offer no definitive answers. But I can suggest some hypotheses based on the Japanese case. Actually, comparative studies are so hard to do that it is quite common for comparativists to offer hypotheses based on one or two cases.

Job security benefits management when the demand for labor exceeds the supply. Management, however, is unlikely to institutionalize job security through labor-management agreements, much less by law. Except in cases of long-term undersupply of labor, which seldom if ever occurs in nature because one can always import cheap labor, management is likely to try to solve their problems within the firm or by asking government to increase the supply of labor. The situation for labor is different. Job security benefits labor when the supply of labor exceeds demand, a relatively common occurrence. But labor can hardly expect government to reduce the labor supply, except perhaps by reducing immigration. Labor can and does request attempts to increase the demand for labor through economic stimulation. However, when labor has sufficient political power over management and government to make effective demands, they are less likely to rely on the vagaries of the market and more likely to institutionalize their demands in labor-management contracts and to seek government intervention. The basic hypothesis is, then, that job security will tend to become institutionalized when a labor surplus coincides with a period of labor political power.

From 1946 through 1949, Japan experienced exactly this situation. Defeat in the war created a massive oversupply of labor, a result of a devastated economy and the return of soldiers and colonists from abroad. The American Occupation supplied the labor power by legitimizing and supporting unions.

The unions demanded and got a high level of job security. Though the hypothesis was developed to fit the Japanese case, we also have some comparative evidence from France. The coincidence of a sluggish economy with an increase in union power provided by the election of France's first socialist president produced something similar to Japanese permanent employment.

A second and supplementary hypothesis suggests a basic elite-mass dynamic, in which elites are forced to live up to promises made to the masses. According to Andrew Gordon's depiction of the development of labor-management relations in Japan, management failed to honor promises made in the prewar period to temporarily appease workers and avoid government intervention. After the war, labor demanded that the prewar promises be kept, and in the early postwar period they had enough power to make it so. In general, elites need the cooperation of the masses. To get that cooperation, they use both coercion and persuasion. The persuasion often consists of rhetoric with little or no substance. To increase or sustain cooperation from the masses, however, sooner or later the substance must be forthcoming. One reason change occurs after wars, whether won or lost, is that elites have a greater need for enthusiastic mass cooperation during wars and, therefore, make more promises. Soldiers are told they should fight hard for their country. When the war is over, the soldiers are likely to believe it really is their country. This dynamic of elites being forced to live up to their rhetoric is central to the evolution of democracy.

Personally, I find these two explanations intellectually satisfying. However, many people are dissatisfied with these simple explanations. Does culture play no role at all? In an insightful review of the English-language literature on Japanese management practices, Haruo Shimada offers a "neoculturalist synthesis." He makes a strong plea for the inclusion of culture:

> In spite of the impressive development of functional analysis as applied to Japanese industrial relations with its massive and well-organized data, refined theory, and methodological rigor, the Japanese audience is still dissatisfied and, in a sense, unfulfilled. Even though functional analysis is supposedly complete and the methodology of empirical analysis is presumably flawless, Japanese

readers remain not quite persuaded. They feel intuitively that something is lacking in the glittering functional analysis — something that is perhaps essential to an understanding of Japanese industrial relations although they are not quite able to identify what it is.[56]

My interpretation of what the scientific approach (Shimada's "functional analysis") can and cannot do differs in two major respects. First, I always tell my students that I am interested not in what they feel but in what they think. It is a question not of what one "feels intuitively" but what the evidence indicates. Second, I completely disagree with the statement that "functional analysis is supposedly complete and the methodology of empirical analysis is presumably flawless." Although scientists tend to be enthusiastic about their methods, scientific explanations can never be complete. At best, a scientific explanation abstracts one clear, narrow variable from a complex reality and attempts to explain the simple basic laws governing its behavior. Thus, Shimada is absolutely correct in arguing that scientific analysis always misses something. Science looks for simple explanations for narrowly defined phenomena. Science does not try to explain everything, only to explain one thing reliably. Science is not magic. Magic works first time, every time, and explains everything. The mystical concepts of culture that I criticize often *are* magic and can easily explain everything, especially after it has happened. Science is difficult. No single study is ever definitive, no matter how well designed. It is the cumulation of evidence from many studies that produces reliable generalizations, and even those results are subject to revision every time a new study is done. Science is frustrating, but it does produce reliable generalizations.

The answer to the question of whether culture played a role in creating a high job security system in Japan is, of course it did. Managers drew upon established repertoires of behavior in the prewar period, when they tried to fool the workers into thinking that the firm was like a family. The trick worked better than it would have in other places or at other times, because workers were partially persuaded by the argument that the firm is like a family. The evolution of permanent employment was made easier by the ready availability of a familial model. Familial models are available in all cultures, virtually by definition, but it may have been that prewar Japan had fewer alternative models because of more recent industrialization and because of the absence of a guild tradition.

Culture adds something to the comparative analysis: if you ask detailed questions about the specific forms job security has taken in Japan, then you need to study the evolution of the practice in Japan's historical context, and a major factor in that historical context is Japanese culture at the time. Culture is context. A complete explanation cannot ignore culture. On the other hand, an explanation that focuses on culture and ignores fundamental social, political, and economic dynamics may seem complete but is not. A reliable interpretation must start with the basic dynamics of human society and add the cultural context later.

Finally, we should ask not only how permanent employment (more precisely, a high-security system) got started but also how it has been maintained. The usual assumption is that it persists because the Japanese people like it. I argue that it persists whether people like it or not. Inertial forces maintain the system, even if most Japanese are dissatisfied. Workers do not quit, because there are concrete costs to quitting. Management does not fire people, because there are concrete costs to firing people. Once the system becomes institutionalized, it is hard to change, even if no one values the system as it stands.

CHAPTER FIVE

Making Common Sense of Government-Business Cooperation

I apologize for having no anecdote to introduce the subject of business-government cooperation in Japan. I hope the idea that government is the natural enemy of business is so deeply rooted in American common sense that a cute story will not be necessary. Americans are surprised to learn that business and government cooperate in Japan. No American businessman would cooperate with government, or even listen to government advice. American business wants government to stay out of its affairs. Moreover, all Americans "know" that government intervention in the economy can never help and always hurts economic growth. This is another of those rare cases in which our common sense about America is mistaken. Once the situation is understood, however, the degree and kind of cooperation found in Japan makes good American common sense.

The Scope of Cooperation

One must begin by defining the phenomenon to be explained. In particular, one must be careful not to overstate the case. Some accounts overemphasize the extent of cooperation between business and government in Japan. For example, Zbigniew Brzezinski describes the role of government in the postwar economic miracle as follows:

The postwar government, staffed largely by people of the same generation and even professional background as the new business elite, adopted a protective and highly cooperative relationship with the business community, with such key governmental organs as the Finance Ministry and the Ministry of International Trade and Industry assuming an overall guiding role, defining — more through consultation than through centralized direction — basic choices and priorities and emphasizing long-range planning, in order to gain for Japan the maximum benefits from economic leapfrogging.[1]

If this were a complete and accurate picture of the government-business relationship in Japan, then the Japanese really would be different from us.

In fact, there are clear limits to the cooperation between business and government in Japan. The relationship has changed over time and continues to vary among industrial sectors and among companies within a single industry. Moreover, the problems Americans associate with government intervention into the economy — corruption, lack of initiative, and bureaucratic errors — are found in Japan. Some aspects of the business-government relationship in Japan are familiar and need no particular explanation. Other features violate American common sense and demand explanation.

The close relation between government and business has produced corruption. If a company can make a profit by bribing politicians, some companies will do just that. Corruption was rampant in the early postwar years, when the government had many authoritative tools for managing the economy. As the government assigned production quotas and prices, official decisions became marketable commodities.[2] Since the late 1950s, however, many government emergency powers have lapsed, and the number of government decisions worth paying for has declined. Corruption is still rampant in Japan and seems to have gotten worse recently, but the style and content has changed. Recent scandals have had less to do with industry than with land speculation and insider trading of stocks. The biggest scandal since 1955 was the Lockheed scandal of 1976, and that involved a foreign (American) company. The more recent recruit and Kyowa scandals have angered the Japanese public as much as previous ones, but the actual influence over public policy purchased in these cases has been much less.

Americans would also expect a close relationship between business and government to produce stagnation and lack of initiative. If companies do not have to compete in the market, there will be little incentive to make a better product at a lower price. And, in fact, those Japanese companies closest to the government have not been the most innovative. Some companies are more responsive to bureaucratic agencies than to the market and, therefore, fail in the market.[3] More generally, the large companies with close connections to the government have not been the most dynamic participants in the Japanese economy. Honda, Suzuki, and Mazda in vehicles, Hitachi, Matsushita, and Sony in electronics, Fuji Film, and Seiko were all closer to the Henry Ford, one-man-show model than to the bureaucratic model we associate with Japan.[4] Some of the most dynamic companies have been small businesses. Small businesses played a major role in the development of the machine tool industry, which now leads the world.[5] Small businesses received aid from the government, but when the government tried to persuade them to merge to form larger companies, they refused.

A firm protected from market forces will not succeed in the market. This is as true in Japan as in the United States. For example, MITI has been very successful in promoting the computer hardware industry but has experienced some major failures on the software side. The government created a joint-venture firm to develop software, but it "turned out to be nothing short of a fiasco. . . . Having been guaranteed government subsidies for the 6-year project, the shareholder firms had little motivation to worry about whether the company was competitive in the marketplace."[6]

Japanese bureaucrats have, as Americans would also expect, made some serious blunders. For example, the Ministry of International Trade and Industry (MITI) thought the transistor had little potential for commercial use. "In 1953, when a small company called Tōkyō Tsūshin Kōgyō sought permission to purchase Western Electric's transistor technology for $25,000, MITI was reluctant to grant approval, citing a shortage of foreign currency. . . . Only after a contract had been signed with Western Electric did MITI, in 1954, authorize the transfer of transistor technology."[7] The company was later renamed Sony, and the transistor worked out pretty well after all. Sony's transistor radios revolutionized consumer electronics.

One secret of Japanese postwar economic growth was the rapid shift from coal to oil as the main source of energy. However, one of the primary goals of the Japanese government had been to make coal the centerpiece of the postwar economy. It continued to try to save the coal industry throughout the 1950s.[8] Had the bureaucracy been more effective and successful, it would have been able to keep the coal industry afloat longer, the transition to oil would have been slower, and Japan would not have grown so fast.

These factors are consistent with the American understanding of business, but other aspects of the Japanese experience require explanation. The large companies that have close relations with the government may not have been the most dynamic parts of the economy, but they have competed successfully in the market. Somehow, government intervention has not seriously hindered the operation of the market. Moreover, the government seems to intervene when intervention might help and to get out of the way when it is no longer needed. The Japanese government "learned which sectors, like consumer electronics, could develop with minimal government aid and which, like shipbuilding and steel, required more government help."[9] Industries in the early stages of development are given government support, but when they become competitive, the bureaucracy withdraws. When the industry reaches maturity and begins to decline, the government intervenes again.[10] It is this combination of effective intervention when needed and deference to market forces when the market is working properly that seems magical and requires explanation.

Business and Government in The United States

As we must not overestimate the degree of cooperation between business and government in Japan, so we must also be careful not to underestimate the amount of cooperation in the United States. Americans are used to thinking of politics and economics as two completely unrelated spheres of activity. Here again, our common sense about Americans is wrong. Our theories tell us that government *should* be kept out of business, but the fact is that business makes demands on politicians and politicians respond to those demands.

What do business interests want from government? Most Americans believe that business wants "to be left alone."[11] Free enterprise is defined as freedom from government intervention. American business opposes government involvement in the economy more than business in any other industrial nation. However, American businesspeople are like any other in that they maximize profits and will even delve into politics if it will make a profit. What position did AT & T take on deregulation of the telephone industry? What position did the airlines take on deregulation of that industry? In both cases, the industries opposed deregulation, because it threatened their profits.[12] What has been the position of the tobacco industry on regulation? They opposed as government intrusion into the market regulation to protect the health of the public but favored regulation to protect the monopoly rights of tobacco growers.[13] Moreover, there are many examples of successful cooperation between government and business, especially in agriculture and military-related industries, that look a great deal like Japanese-style government-business cooperation.[14]

The *tatemae* of American business suggests that it wants government to leave it alone and loves the competition of the free market. Business certainly talks a lot about the free market whenever government threatens to intervene. Nevertheless, much of American business behavior, and much of business behavior everywhere, can best be explained as a desire to avoid competition. Lloyd Reynolds, writing about America in the 1920s and 1930s, introduces his subject as follows:

> Economists have long maintained that free competition tends to promote economic efficiency. Business-men, however, have remained singularly unconvinced. In trade journals and at manufacturers' conventions competition is termed "ruinous," "unethical," "cutthroat," "destructive." The control of competition through patents, tariffs, mergers, trade associations and informal agreements has been a major objective of business policy.[15]

The biggest threat to a company's profits is not the government, or labor unions for that matter, but competition from other companies. In a study of the American coal industry, John Bowman argues that "the principal collective action problem faced by capitalist firms is . . . to organize themselves into stable markets in which behavior is predictable and a live-and-let-live form of competition generates acceptably high profits and economic survival for all."[16] Since the war, American business interests have adopted a different rhetoric, but it is unlikely that they have actually come to prefer competition to predictable profits.

The question of what business will demand from government cannot be answered with a simplistic theory. One must examine the actual self-interest involved, case by case. Businesspeople in different countries and industries may make different demands, and what business demands can change over time.[17] Political economy should be, among other things, the study of what business demands from government and how government responds. My present task is not quite so broad: I am interested in the circumstances under which business interests cooperate effectively with government officials and when such cooperation is beneficial to the economy as a whole.

Debunking Simplistic Cultural Explanations

The most popular explanation for cooperation between business and government, the cultural hypothesis, assumes that Japanese business is more interested in the national good as defined by bureaucrats than in its own selfish profits. The Japanese cooperate simply because they are Japanese. They do not think as we do, and the rules of common sense that apply to Americans simply to not apply to the Japanese. This hypothesis has a long history but can be rejected quite easily.[18]

First of all, as noted above, there are many aspects of the business-government relationship in Japan that fit American common sense quite neatly. Second, there is a lot of evidence that the Japanese do not cooperate naturally and normally. For example, after several unsuccessful efforts to promote cooperation among petroleum companies in the early 1900s, the president of Nippon Oil complained that "the Japanese have the poorest spirit for cooperation, and that is why there have been so few successful cases of joint sales and joint ventures."[19] The Japanese were not naturally cooperative before the war. Although we find cooperation in many places in Japan where one would not find it in America, it is not because the Japanese are naturally cooperative.

The most important argument, however, is that, although many Japanese businesspeople claim to act in the national interest, there are many concrete examples of them acting in the interests of their companies against the national interest and no concrete examples of them sacrificing profits for the sake of the nation. The evidence for the cultural hypothesis is based on the *testimony* of businesspeople. The evidence against it is based on the *actions* of businesspeople. Just as American businesspeople say they are against any government interference but favor government intervention when it makes them a profit, the Japanese talk about the good of the nation while acting for the good of their firm. Comparing rhetoric (*tatemae*), we find huge differences. Comparing actions (*honne*), we find striking similarities.

In the 1930s, Western-style individualism was under attack in Japan and elsewhere as simple selfishness. The idea that people should act selflessly made common sense to the leaders of Japan, and they worked hard to convince the country to work for emperor and nation. Many government officials proposed a coordinated economy fashioned on the German Nazi model. Business leaders could hardly argue for selfishness. Especially after the war began, such talk could be construed as treason. To argue for self-interest was to risk assassination. Businesspeople reacted by affirming the Japanese tenet that selfishness is bad; but they also argued that the best thing for Japan would be for the government to protect management prerogatives against both labor unions and bureaucrats and to guarantee entrepreneurs sufficient profits.[20] Prewar business more or less successfully opposed encroachment of the government into its operations. For example, the militarist regime tried to organize industry on the German model. The key organizations in this effort were the *tōseikai* (control associations). In the machinery *tōseikai*, however, "big capital did not defeat the government and establish monopoly power, nor did the bureaucracy dictate industrial policy. Rather, all affected industrial actors carved places for themselves within the regulatory organization."[21]

The automobile industry provides a good postwar example. In the late 1960s, MITI decided that Japan had too many automobile companies to be internationally competitive. The ministry embarked on a campaign to promote mergers. It promoted six cooperative arrangements, of which two were successfully negotiated. The product lines of these two companies were complementary.[22] The government was able to persuade the companies to merge when it made good economic sense for both companies and often had to provide additional economic incentives. When merger plans did not make good business sense, government pressure did not produce mergers. In 1969, Mitsubishi Motors, displeased with MITI's selection of Nissan and Toyota as the national standard-bearers, signed an agreement with Chrysler Corporation to build the Colt. The Chrysler connection allowed Mitsubishi to get foreign patents and to export without MITI approval. Similarly, MITI thought it had settled a merger between Isuzu and Mitsubishi when Isuzu agreed to a joint venture with General Motors.[23] These companies declared their independence from MITI. Some Japanese companies would rather cooperate with foreign companies than contribute to the national interest as defined by the bureaucracy.

Even when firms do cooperate, difficulties persist. Fujitsu and Hitachi worked on a joint computer development project sponsored by MITI, but they could not agree on which company should take the leading role.

> Neither of the firms was enthusiastic about the cooperation, yet they wanted the subsidies and felt that some type of cooperation, however loose, was necessary if they were to come out rapidly with a full series to counter IBM. Fujitsu's Kiyomiya explained their love-hate relationship: "While above the desk we were shaking hands, below it we were kicking . . . with one hand we were shaking hands and with the other hitting each other."[24]

Similarly, in the United States, Pepsi and Coke cooperate to keep RC and other minor soft drinks off the shelves.[25] Are Coke and Pepsi enemies or allies? Are Toyota and Nissan competitors or part of a grand Japanese coalition? Neither is the case. Pepsi, Coca-Cola, Toyota, and Nissan are all companies that want to grow and make money. If cooperation will make them money, they will cooperate. If competition will make them money, they will compete. It depends on the situation.

Nationalism is one key element in Japanese cooperation. All people prefer to work with those who speak their language and are used to their style of doing business. The Japanese prefer to deal with other Japanese because it is easier. Nationalism is part of the modern nation-state. Although Americans tend to think of businesspeople as concerned exclusively with money, nationalism is also a factor in American business behavior. For example, when Fujitsu managed to obtain IBM patents through a tie-in with Amdahl Corporation, IBM Chairman Frank Cray was upset. "In the summer of 1976, Cray invited Eugene White, then President of Amdahl Corporation, to IBM's headquarters to ask him why he was cooperating with Fujitsu and to advise that he refrain from acting in ways that endangered America."[26]

It is a mistake to assume that Americans are only after the quick buck and have no nationalist sentiments, or that the Japanese regularly sacrifice their own profits for the good of the nation. If you want to know what a businessperson will *say* about the government, ask what country they are from. Americans argue vehemently against government involvement, and the Japanese talk about cooperation for the good of the nation. If, on the other hand, you are interested in what businesspeople will *do*, predict that they will fight to maintain management prerogatives and promote the health of their firms.[27] Culture, nationalism, and other factors all play a part, but self-interest is the best starting point for understanding business behavior.

Bureaucratic Power and Wisdom

The second most popular explanation for successful government-business cooperation in Japan is that Japanese bureaucrats are wise enough to defer to the dictates of the market over their own judgment. Why do bureaucrats intervene only when it is good for the economy and defer to the market when government interference would be bad for the economy? The obvious answer is that it must be something inside their heads. They must be smarter than bureaucrats in other countries. They must be immune to the temptation to control too much that seems to infect all other bureaucrats around the world. The key to Japanese success is the wisdom of its bureaucrats.

This hypothesis is stated most clearly and forcefully by Chalmers Johnson.[28] He argues that the long years of experimentation with state control and business self-control have taught them the wisdom to intervene only when necessary. Similarly, Daniel Okimoto argues, "Instead of forcefully imposing its will on this rapidly growing industry, MITI has wisely sought to convert the industry's dynamism into progress toward public goals by designing policies that cater to private incentives for growth."[29] The power and wisdom hypothesis suggests that bureaucrats have the power to do whatever is necessary but exercise that power only when it is actually necessary. I argue against both bureaucratic wisdom and bureaucratic power.

First, the testimony of the bureaucrats themselves indicates that they would prefer to run things, to have more power over economic decisions. Johnson argues that MITI's golden age occurred after most of its authority to intervene in the economy had been taken away and it was forced to rely on administrative guidance. "Ironically, [MITI's] effectiveness was improved by the loss of its absolute powers of state control following the expiration of the Temporary Materials Supply and Demand Control Law."[30] MITI repeatedly sought wider powers but failed to get its bills passed. MITI bureaucrats acted just as American common sense would expect. They tried to increase their authority.

The advocates of the power and wisdom hypothesis argue that MITI was able to continue its influence after losing its authority. Indeed, MITI was more effective with less authority; but the wisdom part of the hypothesis runs aground on the shoals of the bureaucrats' own testimony and actions. Bureaucrats wanted more authority. Only when the authority was not forthcoming did they resort to administrative guidance and other market-conforming techniques of intervention.

The power part of the hypothesis must also be called into question. All agree that the Japanese bureaucracy works hard to obtain the agreement of those it regulates. But how much power does it take to enforce a policy on which there is a consensus? One could argue that the bureaucracy seeks a consensus because it believes that consensus decision making produces better decisions than authoritative orders. A simpler explanation is that the bureaucracy seeks consensus because it lacks the power to enforce policy without it. The only test of bureaucratic power comes when the two parties disagree. Is the bureaucracy able to enforce its policies against business opposition?

When there is conflict between the bureaucracy and business, business wins more often than not. Issues are seldom resolved neatly, and winners and loser are seldom clearly identified. Nevertheless, the cases of conflict that have occurred support this conclusion. The most celebrated case of business-government conflict was the Sumitomo Metals case of 1965. MITI had issued administrative guidance to reduce production to specified quota, but

> Sumitomo refused to accept this administrative guidance on the grounds that it was the only company among the big six that had met its MITI-assigned export quota for the first half of the fiscal year, and it charged that the biggest operators, Yawata, Fuji, and Nippon Kokan, had diverted some of the steel supposedly produced for export to the domestic market. Sumitomo argued that MITI's base for determining market shares failed to take account of the export performance of the various companies and was biased against the newer, better-managed firms in the industry — such as Sumitomo.[31]

Both Yawata and Fuji were closer to MITI than Sumitomo. This was in part a case of a more market-oriented company bucking the bureaucratic system.

What happened to the rebellious Sumitomo? "On January 11, 1966, Sumitomo claimed that it had not rebelled against administrative guidance but had only sought an exception, because of superior export performance, and said that it would go along with the others. . . . Sumitomo's export quota was also raised. . . . A less important but no less revealing consequence was Sumitomo Metals' acceptance of its first *amakudari* bureaucrat."[32] Johnson interprets this as a victory for MITI. The fact that Sumitomo's export quota was raised is noted but not emphasized. I look at the same facts and see a substantive victory for Sumitomo and a symbolic, face-saving victory for MITI. MITI got the *tatemae* and Sumitomo got the *honne.* MITI got the glory and Sumitomo got the money.

Taken together with other cases, the evidence indicates that a consensus among businessmen is a necessary condition of government intervention into the economy in Japan. When any single large company (or enough small companies) disagrees, however, MITI has very little leverage to force compliance. MITI's ability to elicit compliance from reluctant businesspeople has varied over time. The ministry had considerable powers in the early postwar period of economic crisis. These emergency powers lapsed between 1952 and 1963, and MITI was unable to secure either extensions or additions. After 1963, MITI had to rely primarily on persuasion. Even when MITI had impressive legal authority, businesspeople had the resources to oppose and modify its proposals. Bureaucrats have not been particularly wise and have not preferred market-conforming mechanisms. The bureaucracy has used market-conforming means of intervention because they have lacked the power to do otherwise. They needed a consensus among businesspeople, because it does not take much power to get people to do what they already want to do.

Theories of a Relatively Powerless Bureaucracy

Several other scholars have come to similar conclusions, that the bureaucracy has not played the role normally attributed to it. Some argue that since no bureaucratic power was exercised, the bureaucracy had no effect on economic growth.[33] Others argue that the bureaucracy used to have power but its power has declined in the 1970s.[34] Murakami Yasusuke, reviewing the literature on Japan's postwar economic growth, rejects both bureaucratic planning and individualistic market explanations, concluding that "the weak guidance hypothesis best explains the postwar system."[35] I agree. We need to develop the weak guidance hypothesis further.

Richard Samuels has developed a theory of a powerless bureaucracy from a different angle, by attributing power to private economic actors:

> The Japanese state is a market-conforming player not because it is strong enough to control by other means, nor because it is smart enough to appreciate the efficiency of the market, but because in the development of Japanese commerce and industry powerful and stable private actors emerged who established enduring alliances with politicians and bureaucrats. These same actors vigilantly checked market-displacing intervention.[36]

Indeed, Chalmers Johnson's history of MITI's search for effective means of intervention combined with Richard Samuels history of Japanese big business's search for effective means of cooperation yields a fascinating story. The cooperative relationship between government and business has evolved over time through trial-and-error experimentation driven by the conflicting purposes of business and government.

Marie Anchordoguy comes to similar conclusions in her study of the Japan Electric Computer Company (JECC). "the creation of JECC was not the result of superior insight into the market mechanism and industrial development on the part of Japanese bureaucrats. Instead, it was the outcome of a dialectic between the opposing forces of a government's desire to control and the private sector's desire to be independent."[37] Like bureaucrats elsewhere, Japanese bureaucrats want control. Japanese businesspeople want their companies to grow and want independence from the government, just like businesspeople elsewhere. They do not cooperate naturally. Yet, somehow, they have managed to evolve a means of cooperation.

A consensus seems to be developing on the relative weakness of the bureaucracy, but does bureaucratic weakness mean that government intervention was irrelevant? Two scholars have dealt with the idea that the Japanese bureaucracy might have been quite effective even without power.[38] John Haley has attempted to resolve the paradoxical coexistence of competition and regulation in Japan. He argues that "the pervasive report to informal enforcement in Japan is best explained by two factors: the predominance of promotional as opposed to regulatory policies and the weakness of formal law enforcement."[39] He further argues that lack of legal authority has meant that government intervention has been unable to overcome market forces: "Almost exclusive reliance on administrative guidance to implement postwar policy in Japan has lessened the capacity of the government to affect market forces significantly, except perhaps for very brief periods. . . . The consequence was an *unintended responsiveness to market forces*."[40] The bureaucracy did not overrule market forces because they could not. In fact, the government's main contribution to the economic miracle may well have been this negative accomplishment. In a comparative context, this achievement is impressive. What other government has been able to avoid political intervention to overrule market forces?

Frank Upham has developed a similar, but more subtle and more debatable, hypothesis. He argues that Japanese bureaucrats prefer informal administrative guidance, even when they have sufficient power to force compliance. The bureaucracy uses informal means to limit recourse to other institutions, particularly the courts, thus preserving its position of power. Thus in the Sumitomo Metals case described above, when MITI lost on substance but won in principle, it was yielding on a specific demand in order to maintain the practice of administrative guidance. To fight Sumitomo would have given the company cause to go to court or resort to political channels; and if either practice became common, MITI's power would be jeopardized. Upham argues that the Japanese bureaucracy generally responds to the substance of popular demands in order to maintain the system of informality and illustrates his point with examples from pollution control, *burakumin* liberation, and equal employment opportunity for women, as well as industrial policy.[41]

I agree with Upham's analysis of how the bureaucracy operates but disagree with his explanation of why it operates that way. Upham's theory is a variant of the power and wisdom hypothesis. Rather than wisely choosing market forces over their own preferences, bureaucrats fear the intervention of other government institutions and yield to interest group demands in the short run to preserve their position of power in the long run. This motivation is more credible than wise respect for market forces. And, in fact, bureaucratic power has sometimes led to intervention by other institutions.

Daniel Okimoto points out that MITI has much less money than the Ministry of Construction (MoC) to spend on government procurement. Government procurement gives MoC power over the private sector but at the price of interference from politicians.[42] Similarly, in her study of energy pricing and energy conservation policy, Margaret McKean finds that "MITI was willing to retreat from the headache of regulating the prices of petroleum products in the late 70s and early 80s once it became clear that this task simply put MITI into the line of fire between producers and consumers of petroleum products creating work but no glory."[43] John Campbell makes a similar argument about the Ministry of Agriculture (MoA). Because many of its programs are backed by strong clienteles with strong political support, the MoA has trouble maintaining control over its own affairs.[44]

These examples, however, lead to a conclusion significantly different from Upham's: it is autonomy, not power, that the bureaucrats are protecting. Campbell specifically argues that the MoA is concerned less about controlling its environment than about maintaining control over its own internal affairs. Elsewhere, Campbell argues that the Ministry of Finance (MoF) traded power for autonomy. "Over a twenty-year period from 1955, constant pressure from LDP Diet members (allied with interest groups and bureaucrats from the spending ministries) gradually dismantled the Finance Ministry's control over budget decisions. In effect, the ministry gave up its voice in many substantive policy decisions in order to protect its organizational integrity, particularly in personnel matters."[45] Sabino Cassese argues that several Italian ministries did exactly the same thing, trading power for autonomy.

> The political class uses its own politico-constitutional preeminence (and, in particular, the power of appointing higher civil servants, which it has reserved for itself) as a means of exchange in order to obtain consent of the higher civil servants; the higher civil servants know that they must conform to the choices (and the nonchoices) of the ministers if they want to be sure of the abstention of the ministers for their "career" (in the broad sense). The high civil service exchanges, therefore, power for security.[46]

The Japanese and Italian bureaucracies have similar structures, most notably recruitment by ministry, which produce similar behavior. More important, Japanese bureaucrats do not have to be particularly wise to want to prevent outside interference in their affairs, particularly personnel decisions. It makes American (and Italian) common sense to keep outsiders from messing with how we do our jobs and who we decide to promote.

What power do Japanese bureaucrats maintain by their strategic retreats? Even if we accept Upham's argument that bureaucrats are willing to trade the substance (*honne*) of power for the image (*tatemae*) of control, how can this result in other than a weakened bureaucracy? I also find it difficult to accept arguments that bureaucrats have significant power but choose not to use it. Bureaucrats respond to interest group demands not out of a sophisticated appreciation of the subtleties of power positions but because they know from experience that they would lose if they fought. To fight is to lose publicly. To retreat is to maintain some dignity and the reputation for power. The reputation for power is itself a power resource, albeit a fragile one. A weak bureaucracy knows that if its bluff is called, its power will disappear. In fact, one can interpret a good deal of postwar Japanese history as the successive calling of traditional establishment bluffs.

The Japanese bureaucracy suffered a substantial loss of power to Occupation reforms and then again as postwar controls were dismantled in the 1950s. At first, neither Occupation reforms nor the loss of formal authority seemed to make much difference. Many argued that mere structural change could not affect the more basic underlying facts of Japanese culture. But the bureaucracy was living on borrowed time. Its reputation for power was effective only until someone called its bluff. Japan really is a democracy. It has just taken a long time for both the people and the establishment to realize the fact.

The Occupation tried to give the Japanese local autonomy. The first results were disappointing. Most scholars and, more important, most local government officials believed that the central government still had the power to discipline local officials. Because they believed they could not successfully challenge the central ministries, they made no attempts to do so. Finally, in the late 1960s and early 1970s, local government officials were forced to take desperate measures to solve pollution problems the central government was unwilling to face. They expected the central government to punish them, but they went ahead and enacted illegal ordinances and used informal guidance to supplement their legal authority. The response of the central government was what one might expect from either Upham's or Pharr's model: they told local governments that they had no right to do such things but changed the law to allow them to do so. Illegal ordinances were legalized ex post facto, thus restoring the principle of ministerial authority.

Both central and local officials were surprised at how little the central government could do to punish recalcitrant local officials. Both learned from their experiences. Local officials are no longer as timid in opposing central directives.[47] They have learned to use the structures put in place by the Occupation years earlier. More important, ordinary citizens who got involved in the anti-pollution citizens' movements also learned from their experiences.[48] A new repertoire of contention has been firmly established in Japanese culture.

After a major change, people do not immediately understand the new situation. It takes time. They must learn through trial and error what works and what does not. The Occupation reforms also changed the structure of the relationship between politicians and bureaucrats. The postwar Japanese constitution clearly locates government authority in the Diet (legislature). The Occupation also purged over 80 percent of the incumbents, those who had run with the support of the Imperial Rule Assistance Association. Thus, the Diet had much greater authority than before the war, but most of the experienced politicians were not allowed to participate. The Occupation stripped the bureaucracy of much of its authority, but because the United States chose to run an indirect occupation, most of the bureaucrats were left in place. In the early postwar period, inexperienced politicians with great authority faced experienced bureaucrats with little authority. At the time, many argued that mere structural changes could not change the traditional relationship between politicians and bureaucrats, but the rising power of politicians relative to bureaucrats is currently a topic of great interest in Japan.[49] Once politicians developed the experience and expertise to use their authority, the bureaucrats proved surprisingly easy to keep under control.[50]

The story of bureaucratic control over the economy also falls into this pattern. MITI had powerful tools of enforcement in the early postwar period. When these tools were lost, MITI was able to continue for a while on its reputation for power. When its bluff was called (as in the Sumitomo case), however, both business and government were surprised to find just how little government could do without the support of the companies directly involved.

Granted, the bureaucracy practices strategic retreats in order to maintain power and sometimes prefers informal administrative guidance when they have legal authority. But I argue that the bureaucracy also fears that using legal force would precipitate a political battle that they would lose. It might also result in bringing politicians and the courts into the fray. The bureaucracy retreats to maintain the principle of bureaucratic intervention because they are weak, not because they are strong and wise.

A Nemawashi Model of Business-Government Cooperation

The paradox of administrative guidance is that it seems to be effective even though the bureaucracy lacks sufficient authority (or other forms of power) to make it effective. How can MITI accomplish its ends without power? From a different angle, the question is, How can MITI get cooperation from businesspeople who compete with each other and have no reason to obey MITI's orders? Axelrod has shown how cooperation can evolve in a world of egoists.[51] The explanation begins with an analysis of the situation known as the *prisoners' dilemma.* The classic formulation is as follows:

> Two suspects are taken into custody and separated. The district attorney is certain that they are guilty of a specific crime, but he does not have adequate evidence to convict them at trial. He points out to each prisoner that each has two alternatives: to confess to the crime the police are sure they have done, or not to confess. If they both do not confess then the district attorney states that

he will book them on some very minor trumped-up charge such as petty larceny and illegal possession of a weapon, and they will both receive minor punishment; if they both confess they will be prosecuted, but he will recommend less than the most severe sentence; but if one confesses and the other does not, then the confessor will receive lenient treatment for turning state's evidence, whereas the latter will get "the book" slapped at him.[52]

This game is diagrammed in table 5-1.

Although this example has some unfortunate connotations, the point is that, by following the apparently wisest strategy, two rational prisoners will wind up producing the worse possible solution from their own points of view. The best result is if neither confesses, but each prisoner reasons: "If I confess, the worst that can happen is that I will serve eight years, and the best is that I will serve only three months. If I do not confess the best that can happen is that I will serve one year, and at worst I will spend ten years in prison." Confessing appears to be the better strategy. The prisoners' dilemma describes the class of situations in which Adam Smith's "invisible hand" does not produce the collective good but, instead, produces the worst possible collective outcome. The collective good is best served by cooperation (or collusion) instead of competition. Unfortunately, such situations are not uncommon and arise often enough to cause real economic problems.

One situation that is a prisoners' dilemma is the problem of "excess competition."[53] Japanese companies tend to have higher fixed costs than do Western companies. Because of the practice of permanent employment, the Japanese manager cannot re-

TABLE 5-1.   *The Prisoners' Dilemma*

	Prisoner 2	
Prisoner 1	*Not Confess*	*Confess*
Not Confess	1 year each	10 years for 1 3 months for 2
Confess	3 months for 1 10 years for 2	8 years each

duce his work force quickly or easily. During the high-growth era, many Japanese companies operated with very high levels of debt financing; they had to continue paying interest on their loans, no matter what was happening in the market. During a recession, Western companies cut back on production to match the reduced demand and, thus, reduce their costs. For Japanese companies, cutting back on production does not reduce costs. They have to keep paying their workers and the bank. It is in each company's interest to maintain production and sell its product at any price, even it loses money. Any income is better than none when costs are fixed. If all companies follow this strategy, the market will be flooded, supply will greatly exceed demand, and prices will plummet. This scenario has occurred often in Japanese economic history and is still a major problem. "Fratricidal hypercompetition is to Japanese economic planners every bit the *bete noire* that excessive concentration is to American antitrust officials."[54] Similarly, "excessive competition is often cited by MITI officials as the immediate reason for having to extend so visible a hand in the marketplace."[55]

Excessive competition is a prisoners' dilemma. A company has two options: it can either maintain or cut back production. A simplified two-company game is diagrammed as in table 5-2. The ideal choice for each company is to maintain production while all others cut back. If only one company cuts back, the cheater will not only profit more (or lose less), but it will also gain market share. If, however, both companies follow their optimal strategy, the result is disaster for all. Some of this competitive pressure can be vented through export drives, but domestically the only solution is a collective agreement to cut production. All companies are willing to cut production if they

TABLE 5-2. *Excessive Competition as a Prisoners' Dilemma*

	Company 2	
Company 1	Cut Back	Maintain
Cut Back	Low profits for both	2 gains on 1
Maintain	1 gains on 2	Major losses for both

can be assured, first, that everyone else is cooperating and, second, that the allocation of production quotas is fair.

A strong government could simply impose a collective solution. The government's solution would, however, be more politically than economically rational, and a strong government might impose a solution inappropriately. A weak government can produce a solution through a simple, if time-consuming, process of negotiation. It is in each company's interest to cooperate, if everyone else cooperates. The government can act as a mediator, seeking each company's cooperation. After collecting promises, the government announces the achievement of consensus and firms up the commitment of each company. If there is any disagreement at all, the process must start all over again. The Japanese have a term for this process: *nemawashi*, originally referring to the process of trimming the roots around a tree before transplanting. This is a standard technique in the Japanese repertoire for consensus decision making.[56] We can, therefore, label the prisoners' dilemma analysis the *nemawashi* model of the business-government relationship in Japan.[57]

The *nemawashi* model suggests that business-government relations are cooperative because the bureaucracy performs the role of a mediator in prisoners' dilemma situations. In such situations, companies need to cooperate but need an outside agency to negotiate and oversee an agreement. The government can be effective without power, because it does not take much power to get companies to do what they want to do anyway. The bureaucracy needs sufficient sources of information to check on compliance, but the most important requirement is trust, not power. In theory, an agreement could be enforced with information only. The bureaucracy could punish noncompliance by letting the other members of the group know about the cheater. In practice, however, minor sanctions available to the bureaucracy help maintain the flow of information and compliance with the agreement.

A weak bureaucracy following the *nemawashi* model is *more* effective than a strong bureaucracy. A weak bureaucracy needs a consensus and cannot overrule market forces. Companies cannot grow by playing politics; they must compete in the market. The requirement of a consensus among businessmen makes government policy market-conforming, at least to the degree that the policy makes economic sense to the companies involved. "When the government oversteps itself and makes a proposal that goes sharply against market forces, opposition from the private sector can prevent it from enacting policies that would have led to serious failures."[58] On the other hand, companies may well wish to collude in order to bilk the public, overcharge, and take monopoly profits. However, they cannot collude effectively without the government. The cannot cooperate without a trustworthy referee. Thus, cooperation must also agree with the bureaucratic definition of the national good, thus guaranteeing to some degree that collusion serves the public good as well as the companies involved. All in all, "major blunders have been surprisingly few. It is precisely because neither the state nor the private sector is able to dominate the policymaking process that policies tend to be market-conforming."[59]

The country that has followed industrial policies most similar to those of Japan is France.[60] The biggest difference between the French and Japanese models is that France has tended to favor creating one large company in each chosen field to be the "national champion." For example, Machine Bull was chosen to do battle with IBM. The national champion strategy was less successful, because national champions were guaranteed government and domestic markets. With guaranteed markets, they could make money without making a better product. Why didn't Japan develop national champions? The answer does not lie in the economic theories of MITI bureaucrats. MITI consistently promoted mergers among competing companies. They were seldom successful because the companies were too strong to be pushed around. If Japan had had a stronger bureaucracy, more like France's, it would probably have had less competition and less growth.

How Powerful Is MITI?

I have consistently skirted the question of how much power MITI actually has, posing rhetorical questions like How much power does it take to enforce a policy on which there is a consensus? This question will never have an unambiguous answer, but Frank Upham in his review of *I Was Butchered by MITI!* discusses an illustrative case.[61] The book tells the story of Sato Taiji, the maverick founder of Lions Oil. Sato built Lions Oil by price-cutting and aggressive advertising. As Upham points out, the ease with which Sato made large profits with this strategy implies, first, that market forces operate in Japan just as they do elsewhere and, second, that Japanese markets normally control mavericks and maintain a successful cartel against these forms of competition. Price-cutting and advertising make American common sense. But how can cartel agreements against price-cutting be maintained?

In Japan, as elsewhere, companies that cut prices and advertise make money. Why don't maverick companies simply drive the overpriced noncompetitive cartel companies out of business? What happened to Sato when he started cheating on the cartel? On the one hand, he made lots of money. On the other hand, his competitors fought back.

> Local members of the gas station trade association organized convoys of cars to go to his station. Each bought 500 yen of gas; demanded clean ashtrays, windshields, etc.; and paid with 10,000 yen notes. They cut his hoses, poured water into his storage tanks, blocked delivery tankers, and harassed their drivers. The police were no help. When Sato knocked out one of his tormentors who had attacked him, he was fined 300,000 yen for excessive force in self-defense.[62]

Is this a story that illustrates the power of the bureaucracy? It was not bureaucrats from Tokyo but his business competitors who provided the muscle to enforce the cartel agreements. Indeed, this story adds weight to Samuels's scenario of businesspeople seeking better ways to maintain stable markets more than Johnson's, of bureaucrats seeking better means of control.

Is this a uniquely Japanese story? People in this situation soon come to the conclusion that the cheater needs to be taught a lesson. Violence is a virtually universal reaction. The part of this story that should surprise Americans is not the psychology of the participants but the role played by the authorities. At least in theory (*tatemae*), the American police and bureaucracy take the side of the maverick against the cartel.[63] Cartels are more easily maintained in Japan because the authorities help maintain them (and use them to their own ends).

Upham comes to a conclusion about MITI's power quite compatible with the *nemawashi* model: "The role assigned MITI under the Petroleum Industry Law may be weak in terms of coercive legal power, but it has given MITI both the authority and the access to information necessary to play the role of referee and enforcer in the resulting refiners' cartel. Without this mediating role, it is doubtful that the cartel, even in as weak and vulnerable an industry as oil refining, would hold for long."[64] MITI has enough power to play the role of referee and enforcer, but not much more. Power is less important to this role than information. If the bureaucracy can tell the group that one company is cheating, the other companies will provide the power to discipline the maverick.

Bureaucrats are the referees, not the players. Though we would be unlikely to declare the referees the victors of a sporting event, the way the game is called may make a significant difference in the outcome. Moreover, specific calls may influence the outcome and cause participants and spectators alike to suspect corruption.[65] We would certainly like to know more about how MITI uses its powers and what MITI can demand in return for helping companies cooperate, but the referee analogy at least summarizes our current state of knowledge.

Testing the Nemawashi Model

Several corollaries follow from the *nemawashi* model. If the corollary generalizations are confirmed for the Japanese case, we will gain confidence in the model itself. One corollary is that a consensus among the companies is a necessary condition of cooperation. And, in fact, the initiative for cooperation has come more often from the private sector than from the government. Cooperation has been more forthcoming when the industry involved is in trouble. When the market is not working well, companies seek help. When companies are making money in the market, they ignore the government. Anchordoguy offers a good example:

While the computer companies rebuffed the government's over-
tures for mergers in the late 1960s, the introduction of IBM's 370
series in 1970, the decision to open up the computer market by
the end of 1975, and IBM's announcement that, as of March 1972,
it would decrease by 3–9 percent the sales prices and rental fees
for its 370 series machines, made the firms pause to contemplate
the wisdom of braving the turbulent waters alone.[66]

Fear of IBM, not a natural tendency to cooperate, was the key
motivation for cooperation.

The model predicts that cooperation will fall apart if there
are too many defectors. Several cases in the literature fit this
corollary. For example, MITI designated the electric furnace
industry as depressed and negotiated a plan for reduced capacity,
but "the failure of the electric furnace industry to adhere to its
plan resulted primarily from the behavior of one deviant firm —
Tokyo Steel — which had about a 10 per cent market share."[67]
Friedman agrees: "One large, recalcitrant firm could destroy
the coordination necessary for cartelized behavior."[68] Samuels
provides one of the most convincing examples:

> The Petroleum Associate provides the data upon which MITI
> makes allocations and also enforces them. When objections are
> raised . . . the guidelines are changed. The stiffest challenge to
> PIL-II controls came in the autumn of 1963, when Idemitsu Kosan,
> feeling it was unfairly treated regarding allocations, resigned from
> the association. It took a full year of cajoling, and ultimately a
> higher allocation, to bring Idemitsu back into the fold. Two years
> later Idemitsu deliberately exceeded its quota, and to calm a re-
> bellious, resentful industry, MITI had to grant an additional quota
> to all producers.[69]

The *nemawashi* model also helps explain why the bureaucracy is concerned more with appearances than with substance.
Bureaucratic influence rests on consensus. The bureaucracy must
also retain the confidence of the business community that it
is capable of maintaining a collective agreement. The government must give in on the substance of a complaint to retain
the appearance of power and to reestablish the consensus. Business cooperates in this charade because the agreements are in

their interest. Sumitomo apologized, after it had won on the substantive issues, to reestablish the cooperative relationships that benefit all the participants.

Even when there is a prisoners' dilemma situation and a collective agreement has been negotiated, Japanese behavior is exactly what American common sense would expect. Each of the participants in the agreement has an incentive to cheat a bit, as long as cheating can be kept secret. In fact, that is exactly what Japanese companies do. When Japanese oil companies were brought to court on charges of price-fixing during the oil crisis that followed the Arab embargo, secret company documents came to light. These documents reveal that each of the companies had been refining a little bit more than MITI's administrative guidance had suggested.[70] Similarly, MITI helped negotiate an agreement among television manufacturers on minimum prices to charge in the American market, but each company cheated just a bit and reported false figures to the government.[71]

The model also predicts that such collective agreements will be easier to negotiate and maintain when the number of participants is small. In fact, "the Japanese approach [toward depressed industries] has tended to work best in concentrated industries; in unconcentrated industries public policy does not appear to have had much impact."[72] The failure of *nemawashi* to accomplish a consensus among textile companies on a response to the U.S. demand of export quotas was due in part to the large number of companies involved.[73]

Okimoto has developed a list of necessary conditions for Japanese-style business-government cooperation. His list fits the *nemawashi* model quite neatly:

> For administrative guidance to work, several conditions have usually had to exist: (1) a relatively small number of companies in a given industry that have interacted over a period of time; (2) a clear opinion-leader or market-leader among them; (3) a fairly high degree of market concentration; (4) a mature stage in the industry's life cycle; (5) either a cohesive and strong industrial association or effective mechanisms of industrywide consensus formation; (6) a high degree of dependence on MITI, or at least

a history of dependence; (7) common problems of sufficient sever-
ity to coax individual companies into cooperating, rather than
"cheating," in order to advance collective interests.[74]

Similarly, he gives six reasons for the intimacy of government-
business interaction in Japan:

(1) MITI officials are viewed as impartial and supportive; (2) there
is no tradition of ideological bias against public-private interpene-
tration; (3) government and industry share overriding interests;
(4) most industries look to MITI for some kind of support; (5) the
private sector, on balance, has been satisfied with MITI's industrial
policy; and (6) the advantages of long-term cooperation are perceived to outweigh any incentives for industry to engage in behavior [that is] "opportunistic" or "self-seeking with guile."[75]

Using the *nemawashi* model, we can simplify these lists con-
siderably. The necessary conditions of government-business
cooperation are (1) cooperation has to benefit all the companies
involved, (2) the companies have to be able to talk to each other
enough to reach a consensus that cooperation is best, (3) a government agency must be able to play the role of impartial referee
and enforcer, and (4) the first three conditions must have existed long enough for both business and government to have
learned how to cooperate. Whenever these conditions exist, I
would expect to see the evolution of a relationship between
government and business similar to that which exists in Japan.

My confidence in this expectation is increased by John Bowman's findings that "when bituminous coal operators [in Amer-
ica] accepted collective bargaining in the bituminous coal industry at the end of the nineteenth century, it was with the end
of controlling competition through the standardization of labor
costs, which they hoped would stop the self-destructive price
cutting which their internal effort had been unable to check."[76]
In similar circumstances (excess or cutthroat competition), similar cooperative arrangements evolved, though in the American
case it was not government but labor unions who played the
role of referee.

However, the American government has also played the
referee role. After discussing the Meat Inspection Act, the Food

and Drug Act, and the Interstate Commerce Commission, Bowman turns to agriculture. "Compulsory cartelization has also characterized U.S. agricultural policy since the 1930s. The failure of voluntary production-control movements, led by farm journals and farm organizations in the 1920s, was followed by the passage of several major acreage-allotment and price-support measures, which have continued to define the basic features of U.S. farm policy."[77] Again, we find parallels between Japanese industrial policy and American agricultural policy. Bowman also produces a list of market conditions that facilitate the emergence of a cooperative outcome; his list is similar to Okimoto's and my own.[78] The available comparative evidence supports the *nemawashi* model.

Why Do Government and Business Cooperate in Japan?

The level of cooperation between government and business in Japan is currently much higher than in the United States but not that much higher than in most other industrial democracies. Within countries (including both the United States and Japan), the level of cooperation has varied over time and across industries. If we explain why business-government cooperation varies across all industrial democracies, we will know why Japan has such a high level. The Japan question is a part of the more general comparative question.

In general, we can expect cooperation to evolve when the parties involved will all benefit from cooperation (more precisely, when the relationships are prisoners' dilemmas), when there are only a few parties involved, and when the interaction among the parties is regular and relatively often.[79] The excess competition phenomenon in Japan is a prisoner's dilemma. Industry is relatively concentrated. Business and industry interact regularly. Under such circumstances, it is not surprising that cooperation has evolved.

Johnson has described the evolution of MITI's administrative guidance as a search for a formula that would combine the best of self-control by businesspeople with the best of state control. Richard Samuels has described the evolution of the energy industry as a search for stable forms of collusion to avoid the vagaries of a volatile market. Combining these two stories, one can see Japanese bureaucrats and businesspeople learning to deal with each other in an effective manner over a long period of time. Collective learning is much more than a matter of the cumulation of individual experiences; it is a matter of developing institutions.

The key institutional development occurred as the American Occupation ended and the authority of the bureaucracy over the economy declined. Before World War II, there were few examples of successful cooperation. This was the era of self-control versus government control, as business more or less successfully resisted encroachments from the bureaucracy. During the Occupation, the bureaucracy had more power than ever before or since. The decision to run an indirect occupation meant working through the Japanese bureaucracy; the purge eliminated most of the capable politicians; and the emergency situation gave the government tremendous authority over the economy.

However, the situation proved temporary. As their power faded, bureaucrats searched for other mechanisms to guide economic growth. They failed to acquire substitutes for the lapsed laws because the political parties were unable or unwilling to organize sufficient political power to back up authoritative bureaucratic intervention. An activist bureaucracy that believed itself to be, and was perceived by many as, an "economic general staff" lost power. Rather than give up, it used whatever tools were available. For their part, private actors accepted bureaucratic leadership because it involved no loss of autonomy, because they were experiencing the problems of excess competition, and because private efforts to negotiate and enforce cooperative agreements failed repeatedly.

This combination of the abstract theory of the evolution of cooperation and Japanese history may be intellectually satisfying, but what role has culture played? Although there was a good deal of conflict between government and business in the process of developing a cooperative relationship, and although conflict still occurs, Japanese culture has a relatively large repertoire of mechanisms for producing consensus out of conflict, and the repertoires used elsewhere in society are also used between government and business.[80] Culture adds something to the explanation. Culture also helps explain the specific mechanisms used to promote cooperation and the specific forms that cooperation takes.

CHAPTER SIX

What Should We Learn from Japan?

*A*s *far as* I am concerned, the Japanese experience disproves, once and for all, the old saw that the government that governs least governs best, at least to the degree that economic growth is the measure of good government.[1] The basic lesson to be learned from the Japanese experience is that government intervention can accelerate economic growth. The unfettered free market does not necessarily produce the fastest possible economic growth. Had the government, in the 1950s, allowed the market to direct investment into labor-intensive consumer goods or permitted IBM to dominate its computer industry, Japan's economy would be weaker today.

The second lesson of the Japanese experience is that governments cannot deny the influence of market forces. Policies that go against the grain of market forces reduce economic efficiency, and market forces have a way of overwhelming public policies. Markets must be the main engine of economic growth. The bureaucracy cannot override the market without paying a price, though sometimes the gains may be worth it.

To Americans, who tend to divide the world into two mutually exclusive categories, the market and the government, these two lessons seem completely incompatible. What is the market? Most American students answer without hesitation that the market is whatever happens when the government keeps its hands off. If the government intervenes, it is not depending on the market. However, the most fundamental lesson to be learned from studying Japanese economic growth is that the American commonsense idea about markets is mistaken. There are, to use Chalmers Johnson's felicitous phrase, "market-conforming" methods of government intervention.[2]

What Is the Free Market?

In order to be taken seriously when saying something negative about our American icon, the free market, one must first engage in some shock tactics. Confusion about what the free market means is massive, pervasive, and because it is part of the standard American mythology, remarkably education-resistant. The most effective way of shaking my students' definition of the free market has been to let them explore the consequences.

If we define a free market as one with zero government interference, the best possible business to be in must surely be insurance. I am not talking about the familiar insurance business we know today. I am talking about the business that combines both insurance and the threat you need to be insured against, that is, a protection racket: you need to buy insurance from me because, if you do not, I will make sure your home and business are destroyed. Organized crime specializes in this kind of insurance. If left alone, each of these "insurance companies" will develop private armies of their own, and there will be no government at all. The result will be a perfectly free market. We encourage the government to establish a monopoly in this kind of insurance. We call it *law and order,* and we call the insurance premiums *taxes.*[3]

If the protection racket has been taken over by the government, what is the second-best business to be in? The answer is probably drugs. Narcotics are the perfect product; they are cheap to make and create their own demand. No need to advertise. You can give away your product free to each new customer and then keep raising prices thereafter. When I propose an unregulated free market in narcotics, however, I find very little support among my students.[4] The free market does not produce the best of all possible worlds when applied to drugs. On the other hand, governments have difficulty controlling commerce in drugs precisely because they are battling against massive market forces. Drugs, prostitution, and all the other traditional activities of organized crime are perfect examples of the limits of government power to deny market forces.

My students generally concede the point in relation to extortion and drugs as an exception and argue that the free market is still the best system. However, this slight retreat lays an extremely important base. An absolutely free-market system is no more appropriate for the legal or medical professions;[5] it would allow insider trading on Wall Street. The list of exceptions quickly becomes quite long.

If we define the free market as the absence of government involvement in the economy, then the free market is a bad idea. We need a better definition. We need to reconceptualize the idea of a market as something positive, not simply the absence of government regulation. In fact, markets in the real world are structures created by governments (though not necessarily created on purpose).[6] The classic market is a structure of law and order in which the very best ways of making money are outlawed as cheating and in which the government makes sure that contracts are enforced, outlawing lying as a standard business practice. Economists have demonstrated that, given this structure plus several additional assumptions, allowing the forces of supply and demand to set prices produces an optimal distribution of resources. In a classic market, the best way to make money is to make a better product at a lower price. Selfishly maximizing our income produces competition, which in turn produces good, cheap products for all. This is Adam Smith's famous "invisible hand," which channels individual selfishness into the common good. Note, however, that a government structure is necessary and that the argument concerns the distribution of resources, not economic growth.

For purposes of discussion, let us define the *free market* as the absence of government interference and the *classic market* as a structure that operates like the neoclassical model of Adam Smith and most of the American economic profession. The first point is that a free market is not necessarily a classic market. Economists are well aware of the fact that government intervention may be required to force the real world to look more like the classic market. The usual examples are laws aimed at increasing competition, such as anti-trust laws. The problem actually comes up all the time, however, in a multitude of forms.

One of the assumptions of neoclassical economic theory is *full knowledge:* that the consumer has all the knowledge necessary to make a wise choice. In real life, however, the consumer must frequently rely on the advertiser to tell the truth. Cigarettes used to be advertised as good for your lungs, especially good for young athletes. Truth in advertising is an absolute necessity for the proper operation of the classic market, but it does not happen without government intervention. If it is possible to make money by lying, some businesspeople will lie to maximize their profits. False advertising allows people to make money without making a better product at a lower price. It is, therefore, cheating and must be outlawed. In a free market, lying is an excellent business tactic. We need to regulate the free market to better approximate the classic market.

How safe is the car you are thinking about buying? What gas mileage can you expect? Should the government require car companies to have their cars tested for safety and gas mileage and to put the results of those tests on the sticker for all to see? Is this government interference, destined to ruin the economy? Or is it government intervention to create a more effective market? To me, these are clear cases in which the government must step in to make the market operate more like the classic market. In order to force businesspeople to make a better product at a lower price, consumers must have sufficient information to judge which is the better product.

All the examples so far might be considered market imperfections, in which the free market deviates from the classic-market model. There are also many cases in which real-world markets operate differently, but neither the free-market model nor the classic-market model fits very well. Political economists are more and more coming "to regard markets, not as an approximation of the neoclassical ideal, but as multifaceted arenas displaying wide institutional variations across space and time which are highly significant for the decisions made within them and the outcomes that ensue."[7] We need to look at the actual circumstances in which decisions are made. Rather than asking how much government interferes in this market, we are better off asking how one makes money in this particular market, what kind of behavior is rewarded, and what macroeconomic outcomes are produced. It is not a case of the market or no market, but of the characteristics of the particular market. We need more studies of markets as they actually operate. Johnson argues that "contemporary economic theory is the study of how economic forces would interact if institutions did not exist; political economy is the study of how economic theory is actualized through institutions."[8] If we accept this definition, then we need more studies of political economy.

The deregulation of the airline industry provides several examples of market mechanisms producing strange results. For a while, all the airlines were trying to take off at exactly the same time, and more and more flights were late. Why? Most tickets are bought through travel agents. If the customer says he wants to leave at "about eight," the agent punches 8:00 into his computer, and a list appears. A flight leaving at 7:58 does not appear; a flight leaving at precisely 8:00 appears first, and one that leaves at 8:10 comes later. Because it was a competitive advantage to leave on the hour, all companies scheduled flights on the hour, ignoring the fact that only one (or a few) planes can take off at one time. If more than one flight were scheduled for 8:00, the one with the shortest flight time was listed first. The company that lied the most about how long its flight would take gained a competitive advantage. This was a completely unregulated market, but it produced long lines of planes trying to take off on the hour, and virtually all flights were late. In order to make this free market into something closer to a classic market, the government required airlines to report the percentage of flights that arrive on time.

Is a system in which companies get their capital from a stock market more or less free than one in which companies get their capital from banks? Is a system dominated by commercial banks more or less free than one in which banks are closely tied to the fate of particular companies? The question of freedom from government interference is totally irrelevant. The question is not how much government regulation exists but to what degree various systems promote economic efficiency and growth. When the only way to make money is to produce a better product at a lower price, the invisible hand works to produce the optimal distribution of resources. If people can make money with threats of violence, then the invisible hand produces violence, not a thriving economy. If people can make money by lying, cheating, and breaking contracts, the invisible hand makes the top con artists rich. The important questions to ask are: How does one make money in this market? What are market forces producing in this situation?

Market-Conforming Government Intervention

The idea of market-conforming government intervention sounds neat, but how does it work in practice? Marie Anchordoguy's study of how Japan managed to avoid having its computer markets from domination by IBM provides a convincing concrete example.[9]

How did the Japanese government accomplish this? First, it used the market as a tool of public policy. "Far from rejecting the market mechanism, the Japanese mercilessly, though selectively, exploit it." They rigged the market to produce the desired results. "By creating an artificial market that made the firms view entry as profitable in the long run, the government was able to encourage firms to invest heavily to win a Japanese chunk of the rapidly expanding computer market."[10] All markets are artificial in the sense that they are man-made or, more precisely, government-made. The Japanese computer market was artificial in the additional sense of being constructed purposefully to produce a desired result.

The Japanese computer market was structured by setting up a private joint-venture computer rental company called the Japan Electronic Company (JECC). JECC received low-interest loans from the government and was capitalized with money from the seven participating companies. When a user wanted a particular computer, JECC would buy it from the manufacturer and rent it to the user. When the user wished to trade the computer in, the manufacturer had to buy it back from JECC at the remaining book value. JECC helped Japanese computer firms without insulating them from the market.

They reduced the costs and risks of entering and operating in the computer business to encourage the firms to make the heavy investment necessary to become competitive; and they reduced the number of companies operating in each market segment to help the firms gain economies of scale in R&D and production. Hammered out by the public and private sector, these policies were generally structured in ways that did not completely shelter the firms from competition and that required them to make better products to survive in the long run.[11]

The companies participating in JECC were given a competitive edge but no guaranteed markets. They did not have to be quite as good as IBM, but if they fell too far behind, customers would prefer expensive IBMs to cheap Japanese computers. More important, the seven participating firms had constantly to compete against each other. The market was nowhere near the mythical "level playing field," but it was highly competitive. The market was rigged but not overruled. Even so, there were several instances in which IBM came close to beating the system and dominating the Japanese computer market.

The basic lesson of the Japanese experience is that markets should be considered one of the tools available to governments for pursuing public policies. People used to think that laws were God-given and could not be changed by man. We wanted natural laws, not artificial ones, though we now understand that all laws are artificial. We now want the government to leave the market alone. We want natural markets, not artificial ones. It is time to recognize that all markets are artificial. Some markets evolved accidentally and others were deliberately constructed, but all markets are man-made and can be altered by government policy.

The Market—the Secret of the Japanese Economic Miracle?

The debate over the causes of the Japanese economic miracle and the current "Japan problem" has revolved around the American distinction between the free market and government regulation. Johnson's idea of "market-conforming strategies of intervention" bridges the gap between government and market to some degree.[12] However, if we abandon the idea of the free market and instead focus on the idea of the classic market, there may be no gap to bridge. Below, I offer three hypotheses that Japanese markets are closer to the classic market than are American markets. Japan's government does intervene more than the United States's government; in that respect, the United States comes closer to having free markets. But Japan may come closer to having classic markets. Economists have focused on only one kind of deviation from the classic model: deviations due to government intervention. The Japanese experience suggests that other deviations may be more important. Even though Japan intervenes more often than the United States, the market may still be the secret of Japan's economic success. Let me emphasize that the three hypotheses are offered primarily to break the mold of free-market thinking and open up other avenues of research. I have not tested them. I only claim that they are interesting possibilities.

First, as argued in chapter 5, the Japanese government has seldom tried to overrule market forces. Instead, it looks at the major market forces in the world and tries to ride the wave. It looks at market forces in Japan and asks whether these forces lead Japan toward higher growth. If the answer is no, the government manipulates the market to get better results. Market manipulation is not denial of the market. Americans have been trained to think that either the market operates or the government intervenes. Intervention tends to deny market forces completely. Government regulatory power is pitted directly against the market, and the result tends to be an unsatisfactory stalemate. The market cannot function properly because of the regulation, but the market continues to operate, reducing the effectiveness of government policy. Better to recognize both the power of market forces and the degree to which government creates and can, therefore, manipulate specific markets. This is Johnson's point: the degree of intervention may well be less relevant than the form of intervention. If this hypothesis is correct, then the Japanese government is more active in the economy than the American government, but the market has more often been overruled in America.

Second, as argued in chapter 4, permanent employment creates unified companies that compete by making a better product at a lower price. Japanese companies compete as a unit, not as individuals. Companies compete as units not because all Japanese naturally have a "company spirit." Rather, companies compete as units and have company spirit because they are locked together in the high job security system created after World War II. Employees cannot get ahead by sabotaging the ideas of their competitors within the company. The structure of the company forces employees to contribute to making a better product at a lower price. The Japanese labor market may not be open and fluid, but the labor market has to do less with making a better product at a lower price than with making certain each employee is paid as much as he can earn. Takeovers are difficult in Japan, so that a company cannot compete by buying up smaller companies. Japan has few of the financial mechanisms, such as junk bonds, that Americans have recently become familiar with. Japanese companies cannot make money by juggling financial accounts. They must concentrate on their product. Many American companies have hardly any identity at all these days, and the connection to a particular product has grown tenuous at best. While these American conglomerates may make perfect financial sense, they do not resemble the kinds of companies imagined in the classic-market model and do not necessarily compete by making a better product at a lower price. Even though capital and labor may not have flowed as freely in Japan as in the United States, the key element of the classic-market model — companies competing through production and pricing — may have been better met in Japan.

The third argument is new to this chapter. The classic-market model is based on the idea of market rationality: people maximize their monetary income, or more simply, people prefer more money to less money. However, though this assumption is perfectly valid for the middle class, it is much less so for either upper or lower classes.

The academic debate on the meaning of the middle class is endless. When politicians talk about the middle class, they make even less sense. There are, however, good commonsense definitions of upper, middle, and lower classes. Lower-class people do not have sufficient regular income to plan ahead (read

The Grapes of Wrath). Upper-class people have so much wealth that they need not plan ahead (read *The Great Gatsby*; better yet, read about the current life-styles of the people who mismanaged their savings and loans into bankruptcy). Middle-class people both can and must plan ahead. The advice that comes from rational models usually makes perfect sense to the middle class but is a joke to the lower class and irrelevant to the upper class.

Go to Bangladesh and talk to a poor peasant. Tell him that his problem is insufficient savings. He ought to save a bit each month so that he can invest in this future. This advice amounts to saying, Stop eating for a couple of months so you can send your kids to college. More fundamentally, really poor people live in a world in which the future is unpredictable.[13] Their everyday experience teaches them that anything can happen before tomorrow comes. Neoclassic economic advice makes no sense at all to a person with income insufficient to produce a stable living environment.

Similarly, rich people do not have to worry about the possibility of failure. (A colleague of mine once had a student who, when she heard about the horrible situation of the peasants in Russia, suggested that if things got really bad they could always sell the family silver.) Rich people participate in the market when they feel like it. They might invest a bit here or there, or they might decide to collect antique furniture. They might understand all this advice about savings and planning ahead, but these are abstract concepts, without force.

Only the middle class both can and must participate rationally in the market economy. I would, therefore, hypothesize that market mechanisms work better in countries with higher percentages of their populations in the middle class. Governments in countries with high percentages of their population in either lower or upper classes will be disappointed in the operation of the market, no matter how much they follow the advice of economists. Currently, Japan is the country with the highest percentage in the middle class. Japan has one of the flattest income distributions in the world, very few poor people and very few rich people. It was possible to claim that the subculture of poverty no longer exists in Japan. In 1975, only 17 percent of all nonagricultural households had a savings ratio of zero or less.[14] "All" Japanese have savings accounts. The "salaryman" life style has permeated Japanese society, encompassing farmers and blue-collar workers in large firms. Japan has a middle-class society that produces an economy extremely sensitive to market incentives. If this hypothesis is correct, then the market has been working better in Japan because a higher percentage of the population is middle class and participate rationally in the market.

I have offered three hypotheses suggesting that the classic market may have been the real secret to Japanese economic growth. These hypotheses apply primarily to the high growth era of the 1960s and 1970s. Much of what I have just described about Japan is changing. The stock market has begun operating in Japan, so we can expect to see a shorter planning horizon in many Japanese companies. Japanese financial institutions have been deregulated, and we see more people making money through purely financial transactions that have no connection to any product at all. The permanent employment system is changing. A serious income distribution problem is developing, primarily between those who own land and those who do not. Affluence has affected Japanese workers. They are actually beginning to take their vacations. While many changes will occur, it is unlikely that the Japanese will finally have serious economic difficulties. In the past the Japanese economic system has proven remarkably flexible and adaptable, and it is a safe bet that it will be a dynamic force in the international economy for many years to come.

A New Form of Capitalism?

So far, traditional analyses have made little progress in understanding the Japanese economic system. Johnson argues that "Japan has invented and put together the institutions of capitalism in new ways, ways that neither Adam Smith nor Karl Marx would recognize or understand."[15] I further argue that France, Germany, and even the United States have similarly invented new systems of capitalism that neither Smith nor Marx would understand. (Adam Smith might recognize a great deal of American economic rhetoric and American economists' academic studies, but he would have a lot of trouble with the realities of the American economy.) Japan may be the most alarming failure of neoclassic economic theory, but the need to study markets as institutions is not limited to Japan. Nevertheless, Japan's economic success forces us to deal directly with the Japanese form of capitalism.

Attempts at classifying the Japanese economic system as a different form of capitalism fall into two general arguments: that Japan is a *directed* form of capitalism and that Japan is a *cooperative* form of capitalism. Johnson makes the strongest case for Japan as a directed form of capitalism. He calls Japan "a plan-rational developmental state." Similarly, T. J. Pempel labels Japan a case of "state-led capitalism."[16] While agreeing that government leadership has made a positive contribution to Japan's economic growth, and even that the United States would be better off with an industrial policy and a strategy for growth, I find it hard to believe that the directedness of the Japanese economy is what makes it special. Both historically and comparatively, directed forms of capitalism are more common than relatively undirected forms, like that of the United States. One reason economists harp on the evils of government regulation is that governments are more likely to direct too much than too little. Japan may be among the most successful examples of directed capitalism, but I find it implausible to argue that the economic miracle is due primarily to government direction.

The proposition that Japan has developed a cooperative form of capitalism has greater promise, though a systematic search across time and space would probably reveal more cooperative forms of capitalism than relatively fragmented forms. Americans tend to think of competition and the market as virtually synonymous, but in fact there are always powerful market forces working to produce cooperation among companies. Vigorous antitrust enforcement is necessary to prevent cooperation, precisely because antitrust regulations deny powerful market forces. All economies contain some market forces that tend to produce competition and some that tend to produce cooperation. The specific conditions and structures of the particular market determine which force dominates at a particular time and place.

American history includes periods in which the dominant market forces tended to produce cooperation, but because of the political and economic situation at the time (and perhaps even partly because of cultural predispositions in favor of competition), cooperative tendencies were declared evil market forces to be fought by the government. Teddy Roosevelt gained political support by "trust-busting," and the American government intervened aggressively and effectively to prevent the market from producing the undesirable result of excess cooperation. This trust-busting tradition has been institutionalized in the government and in academic departments of economics throughout the country.[17] Different political and economic situations (and perhaps different cultural predispositions) produced a different government response in Japan. Excess competition became the evil market force that government must fight to control.

Since World War II, the Japanese government has pursued a policy of fighting excess competition and promoting cooperative arrangements. In the same period, the American government has pursued a policy of fighting excess cooperation and promoting competition. The resulting economic systems are thus different, the American system being based on competitive market forces and the Japanese on cooperative market forces.

At this point, it would be easy to argue that Japan really is a different form of capitalism, completely alien to current economic theory. We could easily develop heaven and hell versions of the theory. Japan is heaven: the Japanese have replaced greed and backstabbing with mutual trust and cooperation, producing a kinder and gentler capitalism. Japan is hell: the Japanese have suppressed free and open competition and replaced it with collusion behind closed doors. We could then preach the heaven theory to American businessmen: the cause of American decline is the failure of Americans to cooperate as the Japanese do. Government, business, and labor need to work together to meet the Japanese challenge. The hell theory is for export to Japan: the United States's problems are all caused by the fact that Japan is not a normal country. If Japan would just stop colluding against the rest of the world, the economic growth of the 1960s would be back in a flash. The tough part is keeping American business from hearing what we say to the Japanese and the Japanese from hearing what we say to American businessmen.

No matter how much fun it is to pretend that Japan is a completely different species of a nation, akin either to heaven or to hell, the important result of this line of analysis has nothing whatsoever to do with classifying Japan or identifying Japan's special characteristics. The important result is a reconceptualization of the market. We need to recognize that markets are created by governments and can be manipulated by governments. We need to recognize that many market forces operate in all economies and that competition is only one of those forces. We need to study markets as institutions, not as icons. If we understand how politics and economics generally work in industrial democracies, we will understand how they work in Japan.

The "Japan Problem"

However it evolved and whatever makes it special, the Japanese economic engine works so well that it is creating friction with Japan's trading partners. This is the "Japan Problem."[18] The question is, what are we going to do about it? We basically have three choices for dealing with the Japan problem: give up, force Japan to change, or try to copy Japanese success.

Counsels of Despair

Our first option is to do nothing. There are a surprising number of Americans who believe in the free market so much that they assume that, if you are making money, you must be doing something right. For some of these people, whatever makes money is good for the economy, and Americans should not complain just because they are losing. Others reach the same conclusion from the premise that the market always wins in the end, no matter what the government does. If whatever happens in the market is inevitable, then anything the U.S. government tried to do about the Japan problem would be futile. I suggest that the Japanese experience itself disproves both of these positions. Activities that work to make money are not necessarily good for the economy, and government intervention can make a difference.

Simplistic cultural arguments also boil down to a counsel of despair. Why are the Japanese winning? It must be something inside their heads. They must work harder than we do. We are losing because we are lazy bums who deserve to lose. Our only hope is to change people's minds. If the cultural argument is correct, what we need is a propaganda campaign to get American workers to work harder and American management to be more creative.

Soviet Russia and Communist China have had a great deal of experience using propaganda to get people to work harder. It does not appear to work very well. In fact, I would argue that any strategy based on fooling people is at best a temporary strategy. We cannot change people's minds just by yelling at them. We have to change the real world they live in. Remember, Japanese workers did not always work hard. People (including both Japanese and Americans) work hard when working hard pays off. Clyde Prestowitz makes an excellent case that there are many American managers who are doing great jobs, just as there are many Japanese managers who are not.[19] To the degree that the problem lies inside the minds of Americans, there is not much that can be done. To the degree that the problem lies in the structure of American and Japanese markets, the environment in which Americans and Japanese work, much can be done.

The government can make a difference. If we choose to act, we have broadly two choices: we can try to change Japanese behavior, or we can change our own. We can outlaw Japanese practice as cheating, or we can try to copy the things the Japanese do that work so well.

Do the Japanese Cheat?

My students are always fascinated with the question of whether or not Japan cheats. They want a moralistic answer: Are the Japanese nice folks or not? The answer is that the Japanese are about as nice as any other folks. If we call anything that works so well that it threatens to upset the world economy cheating, then Japan cheats. Governments regularly outlaw practices that work too well, so we will have plenty of precedents for railing against the Japanese as cheaters. But there is no basis for a moralistic argument that the Japanese are all cheaters by nature. That would simply be hiding self-interest behind righteous indignation. Such arguments sell quite well in the United States.

If we persist in moralistic arguments, sooner or later we will find that the Japanese have a pretty convincing moralistic argument themselves: Americans have gotten lazy, and their economy has deteriorated; instead of fixing it they blame Japan. Americans tell us to compete in the world markets, but whenever we start to win, they change the rules. At bottom it is all anti-Japanese racism. The American mind has not yet forgotten Pearl Harbor.

Japan's moralistic arguments against the United States are also rationalizations for self-interest and also sell well in Japan. The two sides of a moralistic argument are usually equally convincing to an uninvolved observer, though each side finds its own to be intuitively obvious. But moralistic arguments seldom help solve problems and often make them worse.

There is a more serious case to be made that Japanese-style economies should be outlawed. Japanese economic policy is a form of mercantilism.[20] Mercantilism can work to make one country richer without contributing to the world economy. The great engine that produced economic growth throughout the free world after World War II was international trade. Anything that reduces international trade could legitimately be outlawed as protectionism.

Unfortunately, our efforts to change Japan have, so far, failed to make a significant difference. We have been able to get the Japanese to change their laws to look just like ours, but somehow the results are not what we expected.[21] One might argue that the Japanese follow the letter of the law but not the spirit of the law; but that is the way laws work, always and everywhere. Enacting a law never causes people to change their ways of thinking overnight. People change their behavior only enough to avoid the newly enacted punishments. We have also found that, when we wish to outlaw some Japanese practice, the Europeans are doing the same thing, perhaps even more. It just does not work quite so well in Europe. The fundamental problem is that we are not demanding the right things.

Should we outlaw Japanese practices as cheating? I do not know. However, if we want to make demands on Japan, we need to study how Japanese markets work in practice, with an open mind not blurred by the mythology of free markets, in order to develop more effective demands. Just telling them to be like us will not work. How can we argue that the Japanese system, which is working well, should be changed to look more like the American system, which is working poorly? If we understood how Japanese markets work, we could devise more effective demands.

Can We Copy Japan?

The Japanese have devised a more effective economic system than the United States. The third option, if we wish to compete with them, is to copy them. One piece of standard wisdom is that we cannot expect one country's practices to work in a completely different environment.[22] It is also well known, however, that this generalization does not apply to Japan. The Japanese are good at imitation, a fact taken as further proof that the Japanese are fundamentally different from us. I argue that both of these widely accepted hypotheses are false. Copying is not that hard.

I often assign students two excellent studies of copying: Robert Cole's work on American attempts to copy Japanese "quality control circles" and Eleanor Westney's study of Japanese attempts to copy Paris's system of policing in the 1870s.[23] Most students assume that the assignment is to explain why the Japanese are more successful imitators than the Americans. They are shocked when I ask them what evidence they have that the Japanese case was a success and the American case a failure. In fact, the cases look awfully similar. If there is a difference, it is that Americans tend to give up too quickly, because they do not believe copying is possible. This is a cultural phenomenon. Most American managers grew up in a world in which America was number one. We do not copy—others copy us! The world has moved on, but ideas remain out of date. The next generation of managers will be more open to imitation.

The best evidence that we can imitate aspects of the Japanese model is that Japanese-managed plants are working quite well in the United States, as well as in Europe.[24] The Japanese management style has to be adapted to local conditions, but that is the way copying always works. The most important local conditions are not cultural. Workers seem to adjust rather rapidly. More important are local markets, especially local job markets. Those people who argued that the Japanese would never be able to export their management practices because their system was based on Japanese culture have been proven wrong.[25]

Part of the confusion about copying arises from the fact that it is impossible to copy anything exactly. Japanese management practices differ from urban to rural areas of Japan. It should not come as a surprise that they differ when applied in an American environment. When the Japanese successfully imitate, they adjust where appropriate. If Americans expect it to work exactly as it does in the book, they will be disappointed. It doesn't work exactly as it does in the book, even in Japan. Sometimes the copied version works better than the original, because the theory, not the actual practice, was copied. Keep what works, discard what does not. No magic necessary.

Whether we decide to try to change Japanese behavior or our own, our success will depend on understanding how the world works. Generalizations that are both useful and reliable are very difficult to find, but when available they work infinitely better than the more emotionally satisfying mystical explanations.

NOTES

INDEX

Notes

Chapter 1. A Unique Nation?

1. When I give public lectures on these topics I usually offer to take side bets of fifty cents each on whether I will be able to make common sense of these two practices. No one has ever taken me up on the offer; but at the end of the lecture, when I ask how many people think I succeeded, the response indicates that I would have made money had the audience taken the bet.

2. Karel van Wolferen, *The Enigma of Japanese Power* (New York: Knopf, 1989). Van Wolferen claims to be debunking myths of Japanese uniqueness and cultural explanations. See his "The Enigma of Japanese Power: A Response to Misunderstanding," *IHJ Bulletin* (Spring 1990): 4–6. He attacks the silly *Nihonjin-ron* literature but fails to be systematically comparative and, in the end, explains the major differences between Japan and the West in terms of Japan's lack of transcendental beliefs.

3. On other dimensions, Japan and the United States are similar to each other and different from Europe. The similarities are often due to the fact that the United States was the occupying power after Japan's defeat in World War II. Probably the best examples of similarities are found in education. Fortunately, Japan has been included in the most recent edition of the classic text by Arnold J. Heidenheimer, Hugh Heclo, and Carolyn Teich Adams, *Comparative Public Policy* (New York: St. Martin's, 1990). This volume argues that Japan clearly falls within the category of industrial democracy. There is no need to create a special category for Japan separate from the West.

4. See, for example, Richard Rose, "How Exceptional Is American Government," *Studies in Public Policy* (Glasgow: Centre for the Study of Public Policy, University of Strathclyde, 1985).

5. In a personal communication, Richard Samuels says that the full mantra goes "small-island-trading-nation-precariously-dependent-upon-raw-materials-cut-adrift-in-a-hostile-world" (hyphens inserted for easy reading.).

6. If one subtracts mountainous areas and such to get a measure of habitable land area, one can make Japan look small and densely populated relative to Western European countries, but there are many reasons to doubt the validity of these calculations. For example, the high price of land in Japan is not due to a shortage of land suitable for building. See Yukio Noguchi, "Land Problems and Policies in Japan," in *Land Issues in Japan: A Policy Failure?*, ed. John O. Haley and Kozo Yamamura (Seattle: Society for Japanese Studies, 1992).

7. I have also had many Japanese respond positively to this argument and ask for copies of figures 1-1 and 1-2, perhaps a measure of growing national confidence.

8. The penchant of Japanese politicians for uttering racist remarks that reveal a massive ignorance of other races has often made the news in America. See John G. Russell, "Race and Reflexivity: The Black Other in Contemporary Japanese Mass Culture," *Cultural Anthropology* 6:1 (Feb. 1991): 3–255; and Robert E. Cole and Donald R. Deskings, Jr., "Racial Factors in Site Location and Employment Patterns of Japanese Auto Firms in America," *California Management Review* 31 (Fall 1988): 9–22. Of course, Japanese ignorance about race should be contrasted with America's record of aggressive discrimination.

Many American students believe that the United States would be better off with less diversity and that one secret of Japanese success is that they do not have to deal with racial divisions. I consider the idea that we would get along better if only we were more similar one of the great and evil myths of all times. People will always find enough differences among themselves to fight and kill over. A colleague who teaches political theory has his students gather in small, voluntary, ideologically homogeneous groups and asks them to draw up the ideal college curriculum. The students all assume that it will be easy, because the religious right will not have to deal with bleeding-heart liberals. They are surprised when raucous debate breaks out. This exercise is a marvelous way to teach tolerance, because it destroys the myth that if only everyone were reasonable, "like me," there would be no conflict. The way to get along is to tolerate diversity, not to enforce uniformity.

9. See, for example, Richard H. Mitchell, *Janus-Faced Justice: Political Criminals in Imperial Japan* (Honolulu: University of Hawaii Press, 1992), 161–62.

10. For example, Nobutaka Ike, *Japanese Politics: An Introductory Survey* (New York: Knopf, 1957), devotes an entire chapter to violence in politics.

11. All data are from G. Bingham Powell, Jr., *Contemporary Democracies* (Cambridge: Harvard University Press, 1982), 22.

12. One could argue that the Narita airport case implies a peaceful

Japan: in similar situations elsewhere, many more deaths and injuries have resulted. Four students died at Kent State. Only three people died at Narita, all of them policemen. The best source is Roger Wilson Bowen, "The Narita Conflict," *Asian Survey* 15 (1975): 598–615. See also David E. Apter and Nagayo Sawa, *Against the State: Politics and Social Protest in Japan* (Cambridge: Harvard University Press, 1984).

13. John O. Haley, *Authority without Power* (New York: Oxford University Press, 1991), 83. See his time-series plot, 97.

14. Ibid., 110.

15. In a group of professors, I easily debunk the idea that what people do a lot they must like a lot by saying that professors love to grade papers; they do it all the time. Most occupations, I am sure, have one task that everyone hates but must still be performed. We cannot assume that just because people do something they must like it.

16. John O. Haley, "The Myth of the Reluctant Litigant," *Journal of Japanese Studies* 4 (Summer 1978): 359–90. For a similar analysis, see John O. Haley, "Sheathing the Sword of Justice: An Essay on Law without Sanctions," *Journal of Japanese Studies* 8 (Summer 1982): 265–81.

17. Japan is actually one of a set of predominant party systems. See T. J. Pempel, ed., *Uncommon Democracies: The One-Party Dominant Regimes* (Ithaca: Cornell University Press, 1990).

18. This conclusion is based on my own research: Steven R. Reed, *Japanese Prefectures and Policy Making* (Pittsburgh: University of Pittsburgh Press, 1986), chap. 2. There is also a historical dimension to this perception of Japan as highly centralized. The American Occupation's attempt to decentralize Japan has generally been considered a failure. The classic work is Kurt Steiner, *Local Government in Japan* (Stanford: Stanford University Press, 1965).

19. The comparative data has been assembled by Iwai Tomoaki, *Rippo Katei* (The Legislative Process) (Tokyo: Tokyo University Press, 1988), 7–10.

20. This felicitous phrase is the title of a book on American government: Hugh Heclo, *A Government of Strangers* (Washington: Brookings, 1977). On American exceptionalism, see Joel D. Aberbach, Robert D. Putnam, and Bert A. Rockman, *Bureaucrats and Politicians in Western Democracies* (Cambridge: Harvard University Press, 1981), 94–100. On the Japanese bureaucracy, see B. C. Koh, *Japan's Administrative Elite* (Berkeley and Los Angeles: University of California Press, 1989).

21. This tendency is not limited to the postwar period. Andrew Gordon points out that most comparisons of Japanese fascism "err in comparing limited Japanese *outcomes* to sweeping German or Italian *intentions*." Andrew Gordon, *Labor and Imperial Democracy in Prewar Japan* (Berkeley and Los Angeles: University of California Press, 1991), 337.

22. The British seem to share this view. In discussing the Profumo affair in Britain, Robin Gaster states: "But lies are the very stuff of politics, as we know only too well." See Robin Gaster, "The Profumo Affair and British Politics" in *The Politics of Scandal*, ed. Andrei S. Markovits and Mark Silverstein (New York: Holmes and Meier, 1989), 73.

23. Van Wolferen, *Enigma of Japanese Power*, 29.

24. I have argued that the description of the LDP as nothing more than a coalition of factions is misleading in several respects. See Steven R. Reed, "Factions in Japanese Conservative Politics," unpublished manuscript.

25. Otto Kircheimer, "The Transformation of the Western European Party Systems," in *Political Parties and Political Development*, ed. Joseph La Palombara and Myron Weiner (Princeton: Princeton University Press, 1966).

26. Chalmers Johnson, "Tanaka Kakuei, Structural Corruption, and the Advent of Machine Politics in Japan," *Journal of Japanese Studies* 12 (Winter 1986): 1–28.

27. See, for example, Robert Caro, *The Years of Lyndon Johnson: The Path to Power* (New York: Knopf, 1982). The similarities between Johnson and Tanaka were first suggested to me by John Creighton Campbell.

28. This and the following data are taken from John G. Peters and Susan Welch, "The Effects of Charges of Corruption on Voting Behavior in Congressional Elections," *American Political Science Review* 74 (Sept. 1980): 697–708.

29. *Asahi Shimbun*, Feb. 20, 1990. In addition, one new candidate tainted by the recruit scandal was not elected.

30. See, for example, Ishikawa Masumi and Hirose Michisada, *Jimintō – Chōki Shihai no Kōzō* (The LDP–The Structure of Long-Term Dominance) (Tokyo: Iwanami Shinsho, 1989), 13. In Japan, this hypothesis rests primarily on the results of the 1949 election, in which major figures in the Socialist party were defeated, while those in the Democratic party were reelected, even though the two parties were in a coalition and shared responsibility for the Showa Denko scandal.

31. For similar cases in Great Britain and the United States, see Bruce Cain, John Ferejohn, and Morris Fiorina, *The Personal Vote: Constituency Service and Electoral Independence* (Cambridge: Harvard University Press, 1987).

32. *Asahi Shimbun*, May 11, 1989, cited in Sasaki Takeshi, *Jimintō wa Saisei dekiru no ka?* (Can the LDP Revive Itself?) (Tokyo: Nihon Keizai Shimbun Sha, 1989).

33. Two major volumes have been published on corruption around the world, but both are much stronger on the country-by-country analy-

sis than on direct cross-country comparisons. See Arnold J. Heidenheimer, ed., *Political Corruption: Readings in Comparative Analysis* (New York: Holt, Rinehart, and Winston, 1970); and Markovits and Silverstein, *Politics of Scandal.*

34. See Judith Chubb and Maurizio Vannicelli, "Italy: A Web of Scandals in a Flawed Democracy," in *Politics of Scandal,* ed. Markovits and Silverstein.

35. Stephen E. Bornstein, "The Greenpeace Affair and the Peculiarities of French Politics," in *Politics of Scandal,* ed. Markovits and Silverstein.

36. Steven Greenhouse, "French Report Finds Insider Trading," *New York Times,* Feb. 1, 1989; and James M. Markham, "Mitterand Friend under Indictment," *New York Times,* Feb. 17, 1989.

37. Aline Kuntz, "From *Spiegel* to Flick: The Maturation of the West German *Parteienstaat,*" in *Politics of Scandal,* ed. Markovits and Silverstein.

38. Bill Powell, Joshua Hammer, and Joanna Stone, "Is the Game Rigged?" *Newsweek,* Sept. 30, 1991, 49.

39. In public lectures Richard Matthews, of the *Atlanta Journal,* has pointed out that many Japanese use similar rules of evidence in evaluating American attitudes toward Japan: anything positive about Japan is discounted as flattery, but when an American says something negative about Japan it is a revelation of the true feelings of most Americans.

40. See, for example, Takeshi Ishida and Ellis S. Krauss, eds., *Democracy in Japan* (Pittsburgh: University of Pittsburgh Press, 1989).

41. Yayama Taro, "The Recruit Scandal: Learning from the Causes of Corruption," *Journal of Japanese Studies* 16 (Winter 1990): 93–114.

42. Students love the idea of "Eastern thinking" and get excited about such works as F. S. C. Northrop, *The Meeting of East and West* (New York: Macmillan, 1960). See also Peter N. Dale, *The Myth of Japanese Uniqueness* (London: Croom Helm, 1980), chap. 1.

43. Arend Lijphart, *Democracies* (New Haven: Yale University Press, 1984), 219.

Chapter 2. Culture as Common Sense

I thank Terry J. Royed for her comments on drafts of this chapter. Since most of her comments were critical, she should not be blamed for any of the remaining errors.

1. Lee Ross and Craig A. Anderson, "Shortcomings in the Attribution Process: On the Origins and Maintenance of Erroneous Social Assessment," in *Judgement Under Uncertainty,* ed. Daniel Kahneman et al. (Cambridge: Cambridge University Press, 1982).

2. Richard Nisbett and Lee Ross, *Human Inference: Strategies and Shortcomings of Social Judgement* (Englewood Cliffs, N.J.: Prentice-Hall, 1980), 31.

3. At the time I thought all Americans considered umbrellas sissy. Later I discovered that this tends to be a midwestern and western bias.

4. Norton Long, *The Polity* (Chicago: Rand McNally, 1961), 140.

5. I thank Craig Emmert for his help in developing this point.

6. We also tend to assume that situations are fair. Magicians say that the easiest people to fool are natural scientists, because they assume that the experiment is not rigged — for example, that there are no mirrors in the box. It is relatively easy to design a carnival game to take advantage of this tendency to assume fairness. Politics are much like games and sports, but we should never forget that in politics, unlike sports, no one guarantees that the two competitors belong to the same league, and no one guarantees that opponents are properly seeded. The won-lost record is much less reliable in politics than in sports. The tendency to assume that the economy is fair has the most disturbing consequences. If we assume that there is no racial discrimination, then we must conclude that minorities are getting exactly what they deserve.

7. Susan B. Hanley, "Traditional Housing and Unique Lifestyles: The Unintended Outcomes of Japan's Land Policy," in *Land Issues in Japan: A Policy Failure?* ed. John O. Haley and Kozo Yamamura (Seattle: Society for Japanese Studies, 1992), 201.

8. Ibid., 202.

9. Sidney Verba, "Comparative Political Culture," in *Political Culture and Political Development*, ed. Lucian W. Pye and Sidney Verba (Princeton: Princeton University Press, 1965), 513.

10. For a related conception of culture as common sense, see Clifford Geertz, *Local Knowledge* (New York: Basic Books, 1983), chap. 2. He defines *culture* as "the shared context of meaning."

11. The worse case ever was a student I had in my early days at Alabama. I was arguing against simplistic cultural explanations for Japanese behavior. I made the joke that Sax Rohmer, the author of the Fu Manchu novels, had said that the Japanese have a genius for imitation. I assumed that no one would take Fu Manchu seriously. One good student put that quote in his essay. I wrote a note beside it saying, "You do know this is a joke, don't you?" and took off no points. Several years later I met this student again. He proudly reported that he had not forgotten everything I had taught him. He remembered that the Japanese have a genius for imitation. The one thing I had tried to knock out of his head was the only thing that remained in it.

12. Helen Hardacre, "Creating State Shinto," *Journal of Japanese Studies* 12 (Winter 1986): 29–64.

13. Lucian W. Pye, "Introduction: Political Culture and Political Development," in *Political Culture and Political Development*, ed. Pye and Verba, 7.

14. See Nancy Bermeo, "Democracy and the Lessons of Dictatorship," *Comparative Politics* 24:3 (Apr. 1992): 273–91.

15. I have found no simple way of convincing young people that culture changes. For one thing, their view of eternity tends to be measured in decades, at the longest. One Alabama student once objected to my argument that culture changes by saying, "Yes, but that would take twenty years!" Actually, I was arguing that it would take between thirty and forty years. I had forgotten that, to my students, twenty years represents a lifetime. Young people have the tendency to believe that eternal problems, like war and greed, can be solved in their lifetimes, but they also think that current fads will last forever. Studying history helps, but the only solution is getting older.

16. One colleague who read this chapter said I was attacking a straw man, that no one really believed in such concepts of culture anymore. After teaching classes for a while, she found use for some of these arguments, and I have been able to show her frequent examples of academics using a mystical approach to culture.

17. I was delighted to discover that the authors of a major volume on the subject find themselves making commonsense errors just as I do. They had both concluded that the city the other author lived in had better restaurants. When visiting each other, they ate at a restaurant chosen by the person who lives in the city. They were eating only at a highly select set of restaurants, but each assumed without thinking that they were eating at a random sample of restaurants in the other city. Nisbett and Ross, *Human Inference*, 260.

18. For more balanced, academic discussions of Japanese culture, see James W. White, "Tradition and Politics in Studies of Contemporary Japan," *World Politics* 26 (1974): 400–17; Ross Mouer and Yoshio Sugimoto, *Images of Japanese Society* (London: Routledge and Kegan Paul, 1986); John Creighton Campbell, *Politics and Culture in Japan* (Ann Arbor: Center for Political Studies, Institute for Social Research, University of Michigan, 1988); Thomas P. Rohlen, "Order in Japanese Society: Attachment, Authority, and Routine," *Journal of Japanese Studies* 15 (Winter 1989): 5–40; and Robert J. Smith, "Presidential Address: Something Old, Something New—Tradition and Culture in the Study of Japan," *Journal of Asian Studies* 48:4 (Nov. 1989): 715–23. For journalistic accounts in the holistic tradition, see Robert C. Christopher, *The Japanese Mind: The Goliath Explained* (New York: Linden, 1983); and Richard Halloran, *Japan, Images and Realities* (Tokyo: Charles E. Tuttle, 1969).

19. Smith, "Something Old, Something New," 715–23.

20. Andrew Gordon, "Japanese History and Contemporary Labor Relations," paper prepared for the Conference on U.S.-Japanese Economic Relations, University of Alabama, March 9, 1988, 2–3.

21. Richard J. Samuels, *The Business of the Japanese State* (Ithaca: Cornell University Press, 1987), 169.

22. Professor Akira Morita, personal communication.

23. The classic work on Japanese culture is Ruth Benedict, *The Chrysanthemum and the Sword* (New York: Meridian, 1967; originally published in 1946). She says, "the Japanese have been described in the most fantastic series of 'but also's' ever used for any nation of the world." Herman Kahn follows up on this line in *The Emerging Japanese Superstate* (Englewood Cliffs, N.J.: Prentice-Hall, 1970), chap. 2. He presents a handy list of such contradictions in the appendix, 191–200.

24. The best example of selling mystical interpretations of Japanese culture is the marketing of an ancient text on swordsmanship as the secret of Japanese success. See G. Cameron Hurst III, "Samurai on Wall Street," *UFSI Report* 1 (1982).

25. Ronald Inglehart, "The Renaissance of Political Culture," *American Political Science Review* 82 (Dec. 1988): 1203.

26. David E. Sanger, "Seoul Is Planning to Convert Its Raucous Politics into Gray Japanese Model," *New York Times*, Feb. 6, 1990.

27. Thomas Rohlen, *For Harmony and Strength* (Berkeley and Los Angeles: University of California Press, 1974), gives a solid commonsense definition to the term: "Wa is not a metaphor. Nor is it some abstract or logical part of a system of distinctions. Rather, it is a quality of relationship, particularly within working groups, and it refers to the cooperation, trust, sharing, warmth, morale, and hard work of efficient, pleasant, and purposeful fellowship. Teamwork comes to mind as a suitable approximation. It is the complex of qualities that makes working relationships successful and enjoyable" (47).

28. Doi Takeo, *Amae no Kozo* (Tokyo: Kobundo, 1971).

29. This point is developed in Lawrence B. Mohr, *Explaining Organizational Behavior: The Limits and Possibilities of Theory and Research* (San Francisco: Jossey-Bass, 1982).

30. See John W. Dower, *War Without Mercy: Race and Power in the Pacific War* (New York: Pantheon, 1986).

31. John W. Dower, "Fear and Prejudice in U.S.-Japan Relations," *Ethics and International Affairs* 3 (1989): 159.

32. Byron K. Marshall, "The Late Meiji Debate over Social Policy," in *Japan Examined*, ed. Harry Wray and Hilary Conroy (Honolulu: University of Hawaii Press, 1983). Oka Yoshitake quotes a 1910 magazine article as saying, "Never since the dawn of world history has the growth of the individual been so respected and material happiness so sought after

as in present-day Japan" (197) in his "Generational Conflict After the Russo-Japanese War," in *Conflict in Modern Japanese History*, ed. Tetsuo Najita and J. Victor Koschmann (Princeton: Princeton University Press, 1982).

33. Sheldon Garon, *The State and Labor in Modern Japan* (Berkeley and Los Angeles: University of California Press, 1987).

34. On *nihonjin-ron*, see Mouer and Sugimoto, *Images of Japanese Society*, esp. chap. 7. Peter N. Dale gives an intellectual analysis of *nihonjin-ron* in *The Myth of Japanese Uniqueness* (London: Croom Helm, 1980).

35. Although the tone is often unfortunate and several examples are misleading, I find much to agree with in van Wolferen, *Enigma of Japanese Power*, chaps. 9, 10. See also Mouer and Sugimoto, *Images of Japanese Society*, 168–85.

36. Hardacre, "Creating State Shinto."

37. Campbell, *Politics and Culture in Japan*, 18–19.

38. Harry Eckstein, "A Culturalist Theory of Political Change," *American Political Science Review* 82 (Sept. 1988): 789–804.

39. Inglehart, "Renaissance of Political Culture."

40. I highly recommend asking students to guess before writing percentages on the board. It is educational both for the professor and the students.

41. Although about a different stereotype, an American student in Japan was once asked whether she carried a gun to school every day. She answered, "Of course. I have a .45 in my purse and a shotgun in my locker." Whereupon one Japanese student turned to the other and said, "I told you so."

42. The best reading on the $n = k$ problem, though not particularly about culture, is J. David Greenstone and Paul E. Peterson, *Race and Authority in Urban Politics* (New York: Russell Sage, 1973), pt. 1.

43. The best one in my experience occurred in an Alabama class. We were trying to explain why some countries are more centralized than others. We defined local autonomy as the degree to which local governments can do what they want, even if the central government opposes them. We tried many explanations, but they all failed. Finally, one student raised his hand and said the answer was obviously "pure political power." I asked him to define "pure political power" and he said it was "the ability of a local government to do what they want, even if the central government opposes them."

44. Margaret A. McKean makes a similar argument and gives nine cases of phenomena once, though no longer, explained only by recourse to culture, in "The Role of General Theory in Studies of Japanese Society," paper prepared for the Third International Conference of the International Research Center for Japanese Studies, Kyoto, Japan, March 5–10, 1990.

45. Harry Eckstein, "A Culturalist Theory of Political Change," *American Political Science Review* 82 (Sept. 1988): 789–804.

46. Samuel Barnes has edited a set of monographs on the cultures of several different countries. Each of them makes good sense and interesting reading, but so far efforts to come to more general conclusions by adding together the findings of these studies have come to naught.

47. See, for example, Herbert A. Simon, "Human Nature in Politics: The Dialogue of Psychology with Political Science," *American Political Science Review* 79:2 (June 1985): 293–304; and George A. Quattrone and Amos Tversky, "Contrasting Rational and Psychological Analyses of Political Choice," *American Political Science Review* 82:3 (Sept. 1988): 719–36.

48. Douglass C. North, *Institutions, Institutional Change and Economic Performance* (Cambridge: Cambridge University Press, 1990), 17.

49. Although his book is basically a spirited defense of rational choice, George Tsebelis gives a devastating argument against the "as if" defense of rationality in his *Nested Games: Rational Choice in Comparative Politics* (Berkeley and Los Angeles: University of California Press, 1990), 31ff.

50. See, for example, Amartya K. Sen, "Rational Fools: A Critique of the Behavioral Foundations of Economic Theory," in *Beyond Self-Interest*, ed. Jane J. Mansbridge (Chicago: University of Chicago Press, 1990). Tsebelis makes the point that the manipulation of tautologies can produce unexpected and important results. Mathematics is basically the manipulation of tautologies. Rational choice and mathematics provide some useful tools of analysis. It is not impossible to imagine game theory playing a role in social sciences analogous to the role played by mathematics in the natural sciences. Nevertheless, one should not confuse mathematics with science. Mathematics cannot replace experimentation in the natural sciences, and deduction cannot replace data in the social sciences.

51. In Stephen King, *Salem's Lot* (New York: Signet, 1975), a story about vampires invading a small town, there is one set of characters who "know" that it simply could not be vampires — there *must* be another explanation. A second set of characters suggests that it is a testable hypothesis and they should check it out. The former are deductive modelers who assume they know how the world works. The latter are scientists. In this novel, the deductive modelers all end up among the living dead. In real life, the consequences of allowing deduction to substitute for data are seldom so serious, but it is usually a good idea to check out the facts, no matter how logical our deductions seem.

52. Tsebelis, *Nested Games*, 40.

53. Ibid., 184.

54. James G. March and Johan P. Olsen, *Rediscovering Institutions* (New York: Free Press, 1989), 48.

55. Tsebelis, *Nested Games*, 40.

56. March and Olsen, *Rediscovering Institutions*, 40.

57. Nisbett and Ross, *Human Inference*, 3.

58. For example, one source of racism is common sense. The members of an ethnic group that happens to live in a particular region is often a highly biased sample: only the poor and uneducated members of the minority group live here. People who grow up in such regions "know" for a fact that "all" members of that ethnic group are alike; they know it from their own experience and tend to be impervious to scientific evidence or counterexamples. The biased sample may well be produced by discrimination. Social norms enforce the stereotypes of each ethnic group. In such a situation, racism can persist forever, despite the fact that it is both scientifically false and socially undesirable. For an interesting example of the power of stereotypes and bias against parental socialization, see David Fleischaker, "Racism — Or Cultural Bias?" *Newsweek*, July 25, 1988.

Chapter 3. A Structural Learning Approach

1. See, for example, Gabriel A. Almond and G. Bingham Powell, Jr., *Comparative Politics* (Boston: Little, Brown, 1978).

2. George Tsebelis, *Nested Games: Rational Choice in Comparative Politics* (Berkeley and Los Angeles: University of California Press, 1990), 24–25.

3. Steven R. Reed, "Structure and Behaviour: Extending Duverger's Law to the Japanese Case," *British Journal of Political Science* 20:3 (July 1990): 335–56.

4. In fact, biologists have applied Axelrod's game theoretic propositions to the behavior of bacteria. If a theory works with germs, sophisticated analysis is not necessary. Robert Axelrod, *The Evolution of Cooperation* (New York: Basic Books, 1984), chap. 5.

5. Tsebelis, *Nested Games*, 43.

6. Norton Long, "Local Politics as an Ecology of Games," *American Journal of Sociology* 64 (Nov. 1958): 251–61.

7. Robert Axelrod, "An Evolutionary Approach to Norms," *American Political Science Review* 80 (Dec. 1986): 1097.

8. Even worse for rational choice is the problem of endogenous preferences, preferences shaped by one's situation, game, or institution. See James G. March and Johan P. Olsen, *Rediscovering Institutions* (New York: Free Press, 1989), 154ff.

9. Axelrod, *Evolution of Cooperation.*

10. On the United States, see Aaron Wildavsky's classic, *The Politics of the Budgetary Process* (Boston: Little, Brown, 1975). On Britain, see Hugh Heclo and Aaron Wildavsky, *The Private Government of Public Money* (London: Macmillan, 1974). On France, see Guy Lord, *The French Budgetary Process* (Berkeley and Los Angeles: University of California Press, 1973). On Japan, see John Creighton Campbell, *Contemporary Japanese Budget Politics* (Berkeley and Los Angeles: University of California Press, 1977).

The structural findings about budgeting has been the only aspect of political science that allowed me to impress my brother. I am the only academic in my family. Everyone else is practical. My brother manages a state park. No one in their right mind would allow me to manage anything. He thinks it is neat to know someone who writes books but that professors don't know anything useful. However, he does have to propose a budget every year and was impressed when I was able to describe the basic budgeting processes in ways that matched his own budgeting experiences. When you have a good structural generalization, you can impress even your practical friends!

11. Similarly, there are many universals in the relations between central and local governments. See Steven R. Reed, *Japanese Prefectures and Policy Making* (Pittsburgh: University of Pittsburgh Press, 1986).

12. Campbell, *Contemporary Japanese Budget Politics,* 272ff.

13. Aaron Wildavsky, *Budgeting: A Comparative Theory of Budgetary Processes,* 2d rev. ed. (New Brunswick, N.J.: Transaction Books, 1986), esp. 19.

Arend Lijphart makes a similar point about electoral systems. Single-member districts tend to produce two-party competition, a powerful structural generalization known as Duverger's Law. On the other hand, proportional representation is a "permissive" structure that tends to reflect whatever sociological cleavages exist in society. Arend Lijphart, *Democracies* (New Haven: Yale University Press, 1984), chap. 9.

14. Charles Tilly, "Repertoires of Contention in America and Britain, 1750–1830," in *The Dynamics of Social Movements,* ed. Mayer N. Zald and John D. McCarthy (Cambridge, Mass.: Winthrop, 1979), 131.

15. March and Olsen, *Rediscovering Institutions,* 113.

16. Ibid., 169.

17. Douglass C. North, *Institutions, Institutional Change and Economic Performance* (Cambridge: Cambridge University Press, 1990), 17.

18. Ibid., 36.

19. March and Olsen, *Rediscovering Institutions,* 63.

20. Tilly, "Repertoires of Contention," 135.

21. Seymour Martin Lipset, "Historical Traditions and National Characteristics: A Comparative Analysis of Canada and the United States," *Canadian Journal of Sociology* 11 (1986): 118.

22. John O. Haley, *Authority without Power* (New York: Oxford University Press, 1991).

23. Susan J. Pharr, *Losing Face: Status Politics in Japan* (Berkeley and Los Angeles: University of California Press, 1990).

24. Andrew Goble, personal communication.

25. Michael Lewis, *Rioters and Citizens: Mass Protest in Imperial Japan* (Berkeley and Los Angeles: University of California Press, 1990), 67.

26. Anne Walthall, *Social Protest and Popular Culture in Eighteenth-Century Japan* (Tucson: University of Arizona Press, 1986), 38.

27. Lewis, *Rioters and Citizens*, 164.

28. See Andrew Gordon, *Labor and Imperial Democracy in Prewar Japan* (Berkeley and Los Angeles: University of California Press, 1991).

29. Pharr, *Losing Face*, 21. Karel van Wolferen's description of the way the police deal with organized crime also fits rather neatly into this model.

30. Frank K. Upham, *Law and Social Change in Postwar Japan* (Cambridge: Harvard University Press, 1987).

31. Peter Gourevitch, *Politics in Hard Times* (Ithaca: Cornell University Press, 1986), 97.

32. See Axelrod, *Evolution of Cooperation*.

33. "60 Minutes" did a story on fraud by such gas stations several years ago.

34. The *Journal of Japanese Studies* 15:1 (Winter 1989) contains a marvelous symposium on social control and early socialization. Especially relevant to this argument are Lois Peak, "Learning to Become Part of the Group: The Japanese Child's Transition to Preschool Life"; and Catherine C. Lewis, "From Indulgence to Internalization: Social Control in the Early School Years."

35. Haley, *Authority without Power*, 111.

36. David Friedman, *The Misunderstood Miracle* (Ithaca: Cornell University Press, 1988), 140.

37. Karel van Wolferen, *The Enigma of Japanese Power* (New York: Knopf, 1989), 319. John Creighton Campbell reports a 1980 cross-national poll in which 75 percent of the Japanese and 41 percent of Americans thought that most people looked out for themselves rather than tried to be helpful, and 71 percent of the Japanese compared to 29 percent of Americans thought people would take advantage rather than be fair. John Creighton Campbell, *Politics and Culture in Japan* (Ann Arbor: Center for Political Studies, Institute for Social Research, University of Michigan, 1988), 6.

38. Thomas P. Rohlen, *For Harmony and Strength* (Berkeley and Los Angeles: University of California Press, 1974), 45.

39. Campbell, *Politics and Culture in Japan*, 7.

40. Aaron Wildavsky makes this point in "Choosing Preferences by Constructing Institutions," *American Political Science Review* 81:1 (Mar. 1987): 3–22.

41. Richard Pasquale and Thomas P. Rohlen, "The Mazda Turnaround," *Journal of Japanese Studies* 9 (Summer 1983): 219–64.

42. For exceptions to the conventional wisdom, see Kenneth A. Skinner, "Conflict and Command in a Public Corporation in Japan," *Journal of Japanese Studies* 6 (Summer 1980): 301–30; and Kenichi Ohmae, "Japanese Companies Are Run from the Top," *Wall Street Journal*, Apr. 26, 1982. James C. Abegglen and George Stalk, Jr., emphasize the experience of postwar growth in the evolution of current practices in *Kaisha: The Japanese Corporation* (New York: Basic Books, 1985). Masahiko Aoki discusses recent changes in Japanese management practices in "The Japanese Firm in Transition," in *The Political Economy of Japan*. Vol. 1, *The Domestic Transformation*, ed. Kozo Yamamura and Yasukichi Yasuba (Stanford: Stanford University Press, 1987).

43. I thank Barbara Chotiner for pointing out the international aspect of culture. The concept of "ideas in good standing" is developed by Donald A. Schon in *Beyond the Stable State* (New York: W. W. Norton, 1971). His concept of both government and business as "learning systems" is quite compatible with the ideas developed here.

44. Samuel P. Huntington, "Will More Countries Become Democratic?" *Political Science Quarterly* 99:2 (Summer 1984): 193–218.

45. While in Japan several years ago I saw an NHK special on American educational practices. They had selected an experimental school in California with open classrooms, no grades, everyone proceeding at their own pace, as a typical example and an explanation for why the American educational system is so much better than the Japanese.

46. Rodney Clark, *The Japanese Company* (New Haven: Yale University Press, 1979), 132.

47. This fact is documented for women in Mary C. Brinton, "Christmas Cakes and Wedding Cakes: The Social Organization of Japanese Women's Life Course," in *Japanese Social Organization*, ed. Takie Sugiyama Lebra (Honolulu: University of Hawaii Press, 1992). It is also illustrated by the complaint of a Japanese woman that Japanese men seem to be "living their lives out of some manual." "Take a Hike, Hiroshi," *Newsweek*, Aug. 10, 1992, 38.

48. Rohlen, *For Harmony and Strength*, 246ff.

49. I owe this insight into American culture to my wife, Michiko. I overheard her explain this while teaching English to a Japanese friend.

50. If you are in Japan, watch one of the English language lessons on Japanese television. Normally the English is perfect, but there are many times when the people say something no American would ever say. Often they have translated a Japanese conversation into grammatically perfect English but have forgotten the cultural aspect of communication.

51. Culture is, in Clifford Geertz's phrase, "local knowledge," i.e., knowledge that applies only to a specific area, not universal truths that can be deduced from theory; contextual detail must be memorized.

52. There is a great old story that illustrates the fact that all customs initially have some good reason to exist but may persist for no particular reason at all. A newlywed wife prepared ham for the first time for her new husband. She had cut off both ends of the ham. Her husband asked why. She replied that she did that because her mother did that. They visited the wife's mother and asked her why she cut off the ends of the ham. She replied that her mother always did that. They visited the grandmother and asked her why she cut off the ends of the ham. Grandma replied, "the pan is too small."

53. See, for example, Ronald Inglehart, "The Renaissance of Political Culture," *American Political Science Review* 82 (Dec. 1988): 1203–30; and Robert J. Smith, "Something Old, Something New — Culture in the Study of Japan," *Journal of Asian Studies* 48:4 (Nov. 1989): 715–23.

54. See Richard Rose, *Inheritance Before Choice in Public Policy*, studies in Public Policy 180 (Strathclyde: Centre for the Study of Public Policy, University of Strathclyde, 1989). David R. Mayhew compared divided and unified government in the United States (*Divided We Govern* [New Haven: Yale University Press, 1991]) and found little difference. He explains this in part by listing factors that "thrust toward constancy" (176). This list would not be a bad place to start when searching for noncultural inertial forces. When one looks at the details of how Japan copied foreign models, one gets a similar appreciation of the force of incidentals. See Eleanor Westney, *Imitation and Innovation: The Transfer of Western Organization Patterns to Meiji Japan* (Cambridge: Harvard University Press, 1987).

55. I thank Steve Borelli for providing this example.

56. The idea that Confucianism goes with economic growth comes from the recent economic performances of South Korea, Taiwan, Hong Kong, and Singapore. This approach ignores not only the time factor but also several aspects of Confucianism that hinder economic growth. See Thomas P. Rohlen, "Order in Japanese Society: Attachment, Authority, and Routine," *Journal of Japanese Studies* 15 (Winter 1989): 36.

57. Andrew Gordon, *The Evolution of Labor Relations in Japan* (Cambridge: Harvard University Press, 1985), 27. See also Sepp Linhart, "From Industrial to Postindustrial Society: Changes in Japanese Leisure-Related

Values and Behavior," *Journal of Japanese Studies* 14 (Summer 1988): 271–308.

58. Ronald Dore, *Flexible Rigidities: Industrial Policy and Structural Adjustment in the Japanese Economy, 1970–80* (London: Athlone Press, 1986), 11–12.

Chapter 4. Making Common Sense of Permanent Employment

1. When I began explaining permanent employment to my class at Harvard, I was gratified to hear a student say exactly what my Alabama students always say. I sat back and got ready to put on my little show. But Harvard really is different. When the Harvard student finished his harangue about why permanent employment cannot possibly work, before I could say a word, the student sitting next to him spoke up, "But the Japanese system seems to work pretty well." My Alabama students had never heard anyone say anything negative about the free market. My Harvard students were more open to new ideas.

2. Thomas P. Rohlen, *For Harmony and Strength* (Berkeley and Los Angeles: University of California Press, 1974), 18. I highly recommend this book for people who wish to understand how Japanese companies work.

3. Robert E. Cole, *Work, Mobility, and Participation: A Comparative Study of American and Japanese Industry* (Berkeley and Los Angeles: University of California Press, 1979), 62.

4. Ronald Dore, *Flexible Rigidities: Industrial Policy and Structural Adjustment in the Japanese Economy 1970–80* (London: Athlone Press, 1986), 93, table 4.3.

5. Rohlen, *For Harmony and Strength*, 79–80.

6. Thomas P. Rohlen, "'Permanent Employment' Faces Recession, Slow Growth, and an Aging Work Force," *Journal of Japanese Studies* 5:2 (Summer 1979): 270. Rohlen lists seven steps taken by firms to reduce labor costs during the recession without firing anyone: (1) reducing overtime, (2) freezing hiring, (3) reducing management bonuses and, in cases of impending bankruptcy, cutting all bonuses, (4) offering incentives for early retirement, (5) forcing price reductions on subcontractors, (6) letting temporary employees go, and (7) transferring workers to sales or service divisions.

7. See Dore, *Flexible Rigidities*, 99–100.

8. Ibid., 93, table 4.3.

9. Rohlen, *For Harmony and Strength*, 14, 18.

10. Ibid., 74.

11. Rodney Clark, *The Japanese Company* (New Haven: Yale University Press, 1979), 176.

12. Robert E. Cole, "The Theory of Institutionalization: Permanent Employment and Tradition in Japan," *Economic Development and Cultural Change* (Oct. 1971): 47–70, quoting George De Vos, "The Entrepreneurial Mentality of Lower Class Urban Japanese in Manufacturing Industries," unpublished manuscript, 54.

13. Mitchell Lee Marks, "The Disappearing Company Man," *Psychology Today* (Sept. 1988): 34.

14. My favorite student was one who argued vehemently in class that Americans love competition and would never accept the permanent employment deal. He later told me he planned to work in the state government, because he wanted the job security. I pointed out that it would be reasonable to conclude from his own arguments that he was not an American, because Americans love the competition of the free market.

15. In prewar Japan, workers complained that they were treated "as dumb puppets, as living machines." Andrew Gordon, *Labor and Imperial Democracy in Prewar Japan* (Berkeley and Los Angeles: University of California Press, 1991), 101.

16. Andrew Gordon, *The Evolution of Labor Relations in Japan* (Cambridge: Harvard University Press, 1985), 33, quoting *Shokko Jijo*, 1902.

17. Gordon, *Evolution of Labor Relations*, 76.

18. Andrew Gordon, *Labor and Imperial Democracy in Prewar Japan* (Berkeley and Los Angeles: University of California Press, 1991), 205.

19. Cole, "Theory of Institutionalization," 147–70.

20. Cole, *Work, Mobility, and Participation*, 13.

21. Jean-Louis Moynot, "The Left, Industrial Policy and the *Filiere Electronique*," in *The Mitterand Experiment*, ed. George Ross et al. (New York: Oxford University Press, 1987), 270. The reforms also brought French industrial relations closer to the Japanese enterprise union model and further weakened French unions. See Chris Howell, "The Contradiction of French Industrial Relations Reform," *Comparative Politics* 24:2. (Jan. 1992): 181–97.

22. Suzanne Berger, "French Business from Transition to Transition," in *Mitterand Experiment*, ed. Ross et al., 194.

23. Rohlen, *For Harmony and Strength*, 82.

24. Ibid., 19.

25. Clark, *Japanese Company*, 118.

26. Kazuo Koike, "Human Resource Development and Labor-Management Relations," in *The Political Economy of Japan: The Domestic Transformation*, ed. Kozo Yamamura and Yasukichi Yasuba (Stanford: Stanford University Press, 1987), 296.

27. Clark, *Japanese Company*, 151.

28. Ibid., 175.

29. Hugh T. Patrick and Thomas P. Rohlen, "Small-Scale Family Enterprises," in *Political Economy of Japan*, ed. Yamamura and Yasuba, 335–36.

30. Cole, "Theory of Institutionalization," 54.

31. Kazuo Koike, "Workers in Small Firms and Women in Industry," in *Contemporary Industrial Relations in Japan*, ed. Taishiro Shirai (Madison: University of Wisconsin Press, 1983), 97.

32. Ibid., 102.

33. Patrick and Rohlen, "Small-Scale Family Enterprises," 345.

34. David Friedman, *The Misunderstood Miracle* (Ithaca: Cornell University Press, 1988), 140.

35. Patrick and Rohlen, "Small-Scale Family Enterprises," 373–74.

36. Clark, *Japanese Company*, 170–71.

37. Rohlen, *For Harmony and Strength*, 80.

38. Clark, *Japanese Company*, 170–71.

39. Cole, *Work, Mobility, and Participation*, 63.

40. Ibid., 62–63.

41. Kenneth A. Skinner, "Conflict and Command in a Public Corporation in Japan," *Journal of Japanese Studies* 6:2 (Summer 1980): 301–29.

42. For a detailed history of permanent employment, see Gordon, *Evolution of Labor Relations*, chaps. 9, 10.

43. Ibid., 126.

44. Cole, "Theory of Institutionalization," 52.

45. Gordon, *Evolution of Labor Relations*, 55.

46. Chalmers Johnson, *Conspiracy at Matsukawa* (Berkeley and Los Angeles: University of California Press, 1972).

47. My favorite line in all literature comes from Mark Twain's *Connecticut Yankee in King Arthur's Court* (New York: Modern Library, 1889): "It was during a misunderstanding conducted with crowbars." The postwar renegotiation of the labor-management deal with "conducted with crowbars."

48. Kazuo Koike, "Internal Labor Markets: Workers in Large Firms," in *Contemporary Industrial Relations in Japan*, ed. Shirai.

49. See Peter Lange et al., *Unions, Change and Crisis: French and Italian Union Strategy and the Political Economy, 1945–1980* (London: Allen and Unwin, 1982); Peter Gourevitch et al., *Unions and Economic Crisis: Britain, West Germany, and Sweden* (London: Allen and Unwin, 1984); and Peter Gourevitch, *Politics in Hard Times* (Ithaca: Cornell University Press, 1986), chap. 4.

50. Clark, *Japanese Company*, 202.

51. Rohlen, *For Harmony and Strength*, 144.

52. Ibid., 92.

53. Clark, *Japanese Company*, 63.

54. Rohlen, *For Harmony and Strength*, 44.

55. Dore, *Flexible Rigidities*, 72–73. Dore goes on to note that this competition is limited to consumer markets that are expanding. In other areas there tends to be more cooperation among companies, a topic I defer to the next chapter. I contend, however, that competition in expanding consumer markets is the key to making the market operate as neoclassical economists predict and prescribe.

56. Haryo Shimada, "Japanese Industrial Relations—A New General Model? A Survey of the English-Language Literature," in *Contemporary Industrial Relations in Japan*, ed. Shirai.

Chapter 5. Making Common Sense of Government-Business Cooperation

The first version of this chapter was presented at the Conference on U.S.-Japan Economic Relations: Critical Issues and Future Research Directions, held at the University of Alabama, March 8–9, 1988.

1. Zbigniew Brzezinski, *The Fragile Blossom* (New York: Harper and Row, 1972), 39–40.

2. Aritake Shuji, *Seiji to Kane to Jiken to* (Politics, Money, and Incidents) (Tokyo: Keizei Orai-sha, 1970).

3. Ezra Vogel, *Comeback* (New York: Simon and Schuster, 1985), 127–33.

4. Kenichi Ohmae, "Japanese Companies Are Run from Above," *Wall Street Journal*, Apr. 26, 1982.

5. David Friedman, *The Misunderstood Miracle: Industrial Development and Political Change* (Ithaca: Cornell University Press, 1988).

6. Marie Anchordoguy, *Computers Inc.: Japan's Challenge to IBM* (Cambridge: Harvard University Press, 1989), 49.

7. Daniel I. Okimoto, *Between MITI and the Market* (Stanford: Stanford University Press, 1989), 65.

8. Laura E. Hein, *Fueling Growth: The Energy Revolution and Economic Policy in Postwar Japan* (Cambridge: Harvard University Press, 1990), esp. 286–87; and Richard J. Samuels, *The Business of the Japanese State* (Ithaca: Cornell University Press, 1987), chap. 3.

9. Vogel, *Comeback*, 169.

10. Ira C. Magaziner and Thomas M. Hout, *Japanese Industrial Policy* (London: Policy Studies Institute, 1980), 47; and Okimoto, *Between MITI and the Market*, 50ff.

11. David Vogel, "Why Businessmen Distrust Their State: The Politi-

cal Consciousness of American Corporate Executives," *British Journal of Political Science* 8 (Jan. 1978): 47. This article explores the historical development of the strange attitude American businessmen have toward government.

12. Martha Derthick and Paul J. Quirk, *The Politics of Deregulation* (Washington: Brookings, 1985).

13. A. Lee Fritschler, *Smoking and Politics* (New York: Meredith Corp., 1969).

14. David Vogel, "Government-Industry Relations in the United States: An Overview," in *Comparative Government-Industry Relations*, ed. Stephen Wilks and Maurice Wright (New York: Oxford University Press, 1987).

15. Lloyd Reynolds, "Cutthroat Competition," *American Economic Review* 30 (Dec. 1940): 736.

16. John R. Bowman, *Capitalist Collective Action* (New York: Cambridge University Press, 1989), 30.

17. For example, an industry's position on government intervention in trade policy varies over time, depending on its economic position. See Ronald Rogowski, "Political Cleavages and Changing Exposure to Trade," *American Political Science Review* 81 (Dec. 1987): 1121–37. See also Peter Gourevitch, *Politics in Hard Times* (Ithaca: Cornell University Press, 1986).

18. The classic statement is Gustav Ranis, "The Community-Centered Entrepreneur in Japanese Development," *Explorations in Entrepreneurial History* 8 (Dec. 1955): 594–607. The classic debunking of the community-centered entrepreneur thesis is Kozo Yamamura, "A Re-Examination of Entrepreneurship in Meiji Japan," *Economic History Review* 30 (Apr. 1968): 144–58.

19. Quoted in Richard J. Samuels, *The Business of the Japanese State: Energy Markets in Comparative and Historical Perspective* (Ithaca: Cornell University Press, 1987), 169.

20. Peter Duus, "The Reaction of Japanese Big Business to a State-Controlled Economy in the 1930s," *International Review of Economics and Business* 31 (1984): 819–32.

21. Friedman, *Misunderstood Miracle*, 65.

22. Magaziner and Hout, *Japanese Industrial Policy*, 77.

23. Chalmers Johnson, *MITI and the Japanese Miracle* (Stanford: Stanford University Press, 1982), 287ff.

24. Anchordoguy, *Computers, Inc.*, 110.

25. "60 Minutes" aired a program called "Cola-Payola," produced by Alan Weisman, on May 1, 1988, that documented cooperation between Coke and Pepsi.

26. Anchordoguy, *Computers, Inc.*, 113–14.

27. See Vogel, "Why Businessmen Distrust Their State," 50–51. The

definition of a healthy firm may well have a cultural component, such as the well-known Japanese penchant for using market share as opposed to profitability. Differences in the measurement of success are, however, easily exaggerated.

28. Johnson, *MITI and the Japanese Miracle*, broke new ground in several areas and set the agenda for a generation of scholars. It is a great book and should be read by everyone interested in the Japanese political economy. That I disagree with several arguments in the book does not diminish my respect for its accomplishments. Other scholars who tend to support the bureaucratic-power-and-wisdom hypothesis include T. J. Pempel, "Japanese Foreign Economic Policy," in *Between Power and Plenty*, ed. Peter J. Katzenstein (Madison: University of Wisconsin Press, 1978); and Okimoto, *Between MITI and the Market*.

29. Okimoto, *Between MITI and the Market*, 168.

30. Johnson, *MITI and the Japanese Miracle*, 240.

31. Ibid., 269. For the same story told with different emphasis, see Magaziner and Hout, *Japanese Industrial Policy*, 60ff.; John O. Haley, "Administrative Guidance versus Formal Regulation," in *Law and Trade Issues of the Japanese Economy*, ed. Gary R. Saxonhouse and Kozo Yamamura (Seattle: University of Washington Press, 1986), 117ff.; and Frank K. Upham, *Law and Social Change in Japan* (Cambridge: Harvard University Press, 1987), 176ff.

32. Johnson, *MITI and the Japanese Miracle*, 271.

33. See, for example, Fukushima Kiyohiko, "Public Use of Private Interests: Japan's Industrial Policy," in *National Industrial Policies*, ed. Robert E. Driscoll and Jack N. Behrman (Oelgeschlager, Gunn and Hain, 1984); and Merton J. Peck, Richard C. Leven and Akira Goto, "Picking Losers: Public Policy Toward Declining Industries in Japan," *Journal of Japanese Studies* 13 (Winter 1987): 79-123.

34. See, for example, T. J. Pempel, "The Unbundling of 'Japan, Inc.,'" *Journal of Japanese Studies* 13 (Summer 1987): 271-306, and Mototada Kikkawa, "Shipbuilding, Motor Cars and Semiconductors: The Diminishing Role of Industrial Policy in Japan," in *Europe's Industries: Public and Private Strategies for Change*, ed. Geoffrey Shepherd et al. (London: Frances Pinter, 1983).

35. Murakami Yasusuke, "The Japanese Model of Political Economy," in *The Political Economy of Japan*, ed. Kozo Yamamura and Yasukichi Yasuba (Stanford: Stanford University Press, 1987).

36. Samuels, *Business of the Japanese State*, 2.

37. Anchordoguy, *Computers, Inc.*, 60.

38. The idea that weakness can lead to success and power to failure sounds strange, but such cases come up relatively often. For example, Sidney Tarrow argues that one secret of Italy's Christian Democratic party's

longevity is its weakness. See his "Maintaining Hegemony in Italy: The Softer They Rise, the Slower They Fall!" in *Uncommon Democracies: The One-Party Dominant Regimes*, ed. T. J. Pempel (Ithaca: Cornell University Press, 1990), esp. 319ff.

39. Haley, "Administrative Guidance," 111.

40. Ibid., 120.

41. Upham, *Law and Soocial Change in Japan*.

42. Okimoto, *Between MITI and the Market*, 99.

43. Margaret McKean, "State Strength and the Public Interest in Japan," unpublished manuscript, 8.

44. John Creighton Campbell, *Contemporary Japanese Budget Politics* (Berkeley and Los Angeles: University of California Press, 1977), 25.

45. John Creighton Campbell, "Democracy and Bureaucracy in Japan," in *Democracy in Japan*, ed. Takeshi Ishida and Ellis S. Krauss (Pittsburgh: University of Pittsburgh Press, 1989), 133.

46. Sabino Cassese, "The Higher Civil Service in Italy," in *Bureaucrats and Policy Making*, ed. Ezra Suleiman (New York: Holmes and Meier, 1984), 46.

47. Steven R. Reed, *Japanese Prefectures and Policy Making* (Pittsburgh: The University of Pittsburgh Press, 1986), chap. 2.

48. Margaret A. McKean, "Political Socialization Through Citizens' Movements," in *Political Opposition and Local Politics in Japan*, ed. Kurt Steiner et al. (Princeton: Princeton University Press, 1980).

49. See, for example, Yamaguchi Jiro, *Ittō Shihai Taisei no Hōhai* (The Fall of One-Party Dominance) (Tokyo: Iwanami Shoten, 1989), 143ff.

50. Tanaka Kakuei was one of the first to discover how easy it is for politicians to handle bureaucrats. See Chalmers Johnson, "Tanaka Kakuei, Structural Corruption, and the Advent of Machine Politics in Japan," *Journal of Japanese Studies* 12:1 (Winter 1986): 6, 27–28.

51. Robert Axelrod, *The Evolution of Cooperation* (New York: Basic Books, 1984).

52. R. Duncan Luce and Howard Raifa, *Games and Decisions* (John Wiley and Sons, 1957), 95.

53. See James Abegglen and William V. Rapp, "Japanese Managerial Behavior and Excessive Competition," *Developing Economies* (Dec. 1970): 427–43; and Kozo Yamamura and Jan Vandenberg, "Japan's Rapid Growth Policy on Trial: The Television Case," in *Law and Trade Issues*, ed. Saxonhouse and Yamamura, 240ff. For a similar analysis based on American and European examples, see John R. Bowman, *Capitalist Collective Action* (New York: Cambridge University Press, 1989), 9–12.

54. Samuels, *Business of the Japanese State*, 262.

55. Okimoto, *Between MITI and the Market*, 38.

56. On what Japanese consensus decision making means, see John C.

Campbell, "Policy Conflict and Its Resolution within the Governmental System," in *Conflict in Japan*, ed. Ellis Krauss et al. (Honolulu: University of Hawaii Press, 1984).

57. Although *nemawashi* is not usually thought of as a standard part of the American repertoire for decision making, it may be more common than we think in America. I have certainly seen it practiced in America. At one faculty meeting, we had resolved all of the major issues but found it impossible to reach a decision on the number of hours that graduate students should have to finish their exams. Academics will recognize the syndrome of spending more time on minor than major issues. The chair finally let the issue drop without adjourning the meeting. During the dinner that followed the meeting, the chair got up and walked around the table three times, stopping to talk to each of the major participants in the debate. Finally, he announced that he seemed to have a consensus. If there were no objection he would proceed on that basis. I happened to see the chair after the meeting, and he apologized for his dismal lack of leadership. I told him that it was the best example of Japanese leadership I had ever seen.

Similarly, a Japanese friend had been looking forward to seeing American-style decision making in action during his two-year stay in the United States. After watching two different political science departments make decisions, he still had not seen any American-style decision making. All he saw was Japanese-style decision making.

58. Anchordoguy, *Computers, Inc.*, 180.

59. Ibid., 181.

60. On French industrial policy, see William J. Adams and Christian Stoffaes, eds. *French Industrial Policy* (Washington: Brookings, 1986).

61. Frank K. Upham, "The Man Who Would Import: A Cautionary Tale about Bucking the System in Japan," *Journal of Japanese Studies* 17:2 (Summer 1991): 323–43.

62. Ibid., 328.

63. American authorities probably do more to squelch the efforts of mavericks in business than Americans would like to believe. One can better appreciate how the Japanese market works by watching the movie, *Tucker*, about a maverick auto manufacturer in Detroit.

64. Upham, "The Man Who Would Import," 342.

65. This analogy was suggested by McKean, "State Strength and the Public Interest in Japan," 3.

66. Anchordoguy, *Computers, Inc.*, 106.

67. Peck et al., "Picking Losers," 98.

68. Friedman, *Misunderstood Miracle*, 49.

69. Samuels, *Business of the Japanese State*, 203.

70. Takashi Wakiyama, "The Implementation and Effectiveness of

MITI's Administrative Guidance," in *Comparative Government-Industry Relations*, ed. Wilks and Wright.

71. Yamamura and Vandenberg, "Japan's Rapid Growth Policy," 261.

72. Peck et al., "Picking Losers," 82.

73. Otake Hideo, *Gendai Nihon no Seiji Kenryoku Keizai Kenryoku* (Political Power and Economic Power in Modern Japan) (Tokyo: Sanichi Shobo, 1979).

74. Okimoto, *Between MITI and the Market*, 94.

75. Ibid., 156.

76. Bowman, *Capitalist Collective Action*, 59.

77. Ibid., 66–67.

78. Ibid., 17–23.

79. Axelrod, *Evolution of Cooperation*.

80. On the concrete ways Japanese produce consensus within the government, see Campbell, "Policy Conflict and Its Resolution," in *Conflict in Japan*, ed. Krauss et al. I also highly recommend the rest of his volume.

Chapter 6. What Should We Learn from Japan?

1. It is quite reasonable to take the philosophical position that the government that governs least *defines* the best government. One could argue that governing least provides the most freedom and that freedom is more important than economic growth.

2. Chalmers Johnson, *MITI and the Japanese Miracle* (Stanford: Stanford University Press, 1982), 317ff.

3. This probably sounds fanciful to most readers, but there is a good historical basis for this view of the state. See Charles Tilly, "War Making and State Making as Organized Crime," in *Bringing the State Back In*, ed. Peter Evans and Theda Skocpol (New York: Cambridge University Press, 1985).

4. There is an excellent case for legalizing drugs based in large part on a realistic assessment of the market forces involved, but the case is for a regulated and taxed market, not for a free market.

5. Presumably, many of the patent medicines sold by traveling salesmen in the Old West contained alcohol and cocaine. If the market were unregulated today, would these products be found on supermarket shelves?

6. The best work on markets as structures is Peter Hall, *Governing the Economy: The Politics of State Intervention in Britain and France* (New York: Oxford University Press, 1986).

7. Peter A. Hall, in a book review essay, *Comparative Political Studies* 23:4 (Jan. 1991): 546.

8. Chalmers Johnson, "Studies of Japanese Political Economy: A Crisis in Theory," *Japan Foundation Newsletter* 16:3 (Dec. 1988): 2.

9. Marie Anchordoguy, *Computers, Inc.: Japan's Challenge to IBM* (Cambridge: Harvard University Press, 1989).

10. Ibid., 8, 91.

11. Ibid., 3.

12. Johnson, *MITI and the Japanese Miracle*, 317. See also Daniel I. Okimoto, *Between MITI and the Market* (Stanford: Stanford University Press, 1989), for attempts to construct concepts that bridge the gap between government and market.

13. F. G. Bailey, "The Peasant View of a Bad Life," *Advancement of Sciences* 23 (Dec. 1966): 399–409.

14. See Murakami Yasuske, "The Age of New Middle Mass Politics: The Case of Japan," *Journal of Japanese Studies* 8:1 (Winter 1982): 29–72; Margaret A. McKean, "Equality," in *Democracy in Japan*, ed. Takeshi Ishida and Ellis S. Krauss (Pittsburgh: University of Pittsburgh Press, 1989); Masayoshi Chubachi and Koji Taira, "Poverty in Modern Japan: Perceptions and Realities," in *Japanese Industrialization and Its Social Consequences*, ed. Hugh Patrick (Berkeley and Los Angeles: University of California Press, 1976), 397; Toshiyuki Mizoguchi and Noriyuki Takayama, *Equity and Poverty Under Conditions of Rapid Economic Growth: The Japanese Experience* (Tokyo: Kinokuniya, 1984), 183, table 4.18.

15. Chalmers Johnson, "How to Think About Economic Competition from Japan," *Journal of Japanese Studies* 13 (Summer 1987): 420.

16. Johnson, *MITI and the Japanese Miracle*, chap. 9; T. J. Pempel, *Policy and Politics in Japan: Creative Conservatism* (Philadelphia: Temple University Press, 1982), chap. 2.

17. Politicians are fond of noting that economists tend to disagree with each other, as in "If you lined up all the economists in the world end to end, they still could not reach a conclusion." Nevertheless, American economists are more likely to agree on advice to the government than scholars from any other discipline that advises the government, certainly any other social science discipline. When the Hawley-Smoot Tariff Act of 1930 was under consideration, "about a thousand economists, virtually the entire American community of professional economists at the time, signed a petition opposing the tariff. Peter Gourevitch, *Politics in Hard Times* (Ithaca: Cornell University Press, 1986), 54. Similarly, the deregulation movement in the Carter and Reagan administrations was accelerated because no respectable economist could be found to oppose the idea. See Martha Derthick and Paul J. Quirk, *The Politics of Deregulation* (Washington: Brookings, 1985).

18. Karel van Wolferen, *The Enigma of Japanese Power*, chapter 1.

19. Clyde Prestowitz, *Trading Places* (New York: Basic Books, 1988), esp. chap. 7.

20. For definitions and historical analysis of different types of national economic policies, see Gourevitch, *Politics in Hard Times*, esp. 50ff.

21. See Prestowitz, *Trading Places*, esp. 169.

22. Richard Rose offers a fascinating counterargument in *Prospective Evaluation Through Comparative Analysis*, Studies in Public Policy 182 (Centre for the Study of Public Policy, 1990).

23. Robert Cole, "Learning from the Japanese: Prospects and Pitfalls," *Management Review* (Sept. 1980): 23–42; Eleanor Westney, "The Emulation of Western Organizations in Meiji Japan: The Case of the Paris Prefecture of Police and the Keishi-cho," *Journal of Japanese Studies* 8 (Summer 1982): 00. I also recommend Eleanor Westney's book, *Imitation and Innovation: The Transfer of Western Organization Patterns to Meiji Japan* (Cambridge: Harvard University Press, 1987), as a theoretical work on how copying works in practice. The cases are all Japanese, but the theory should work anywhere.

24. See, for example, Richard Tanner Johnson and William G. Ouchi, "Made in America (under Japanese management)," *Harvard Business Review* (Sept.–Oct. 1978): 61–69.

25. Chalmers Johnson makes this point in "Japanese-Style Management in America," *California Management Review* (Summer 1988): 40.

Index

Abegglen, James, 78
Advertising, 139
American agricultural policy, 133
American blacks, 40
American classrooms, 59
American coal industry, 110
American common sense, 3–4, 17, 59,
   68, 77–78, 81–83, 106, 131
American companies: compared to
   Japanese companies, 29, 82, 84,
   92–95, 98–100, 144; competition
   in, 98–101; firings and layoffs by,
   92; quitting, 88–90; relationship of
   workers and managers in, 83
American culture, 59, 66
American democracy, 17–18
American economy, 146–48
American labor unions, 132
American markets, 142, 148
American social structure, 59
Americans: Japanese stereotypes of,
   151; variation among, 66; view of
   politicians, 17, 39–40
American-style business strategy, 58
American-style communications, 64–
   65, 67–68, 70–71
American-style decision making, 35
American-style management, 62–63;
   in Japan, 94–95; Japanese view of,
   92–93
American workers, 151
Anchordoguy, Marie, 118, 129–30
AT&T, 110
Auroux laws (France), 87

Autonomy, 60, 91–92, 102
Axelrod, Robert, 123

Banks, 140
Bismarck, Otto van, 57
Bowman, John, 111, 132–33
Budgeting, 51–52
Burakumin, 56, 119
Bureaucracy: conflict with business,
   116; in Japan, 114–15, 119–21,
   122–23, 134; and market forces,
   115, 117–19, 125–29, 136–37
Bureaucratic power, 115–16, 117–23,
   126–29
Business strategy, 57–59
Business-government conflict in
   Japan, 116
Business-government cooperation, 3,
   111, 113–14, 118, 129–30, 132–34;
   in Japan, 106–09, 111–14, 118,
   126–27, 131–32, 133–35; in the
   U.S., 109–10, 112, 132–33
Brzezinski, Zbigniew, 106–07

Campbell, John Creighton, 38, 52,
   61–62, 120
Capitalism, 146–49
Cassese, Sabino, 120
China, 9, 36, 150
Chrysler Corporation, 63, 113
Classic market, 138–40, 143–44,
   146
Coca-Cola, 113
Cole, Robert, 85, 152

Pitt Series in Policy and Institutional Studies
Bert A. Rockman, Editor

Congress and Economic Policymaking
Darrell M. West

Democracy in Japan
Takeshi Ishida and Ellis S. Krauss, Editors

Demographic Change and the American Future
R. Scott Fosler, William Alonso, Jack A. Meyer, and Rosemary Kern

The Development of the Dutch Welfare State: From Workers' Insurance to Universal Entitlement
Robert H. Cox

Economic Decline and Political Change: Canada, Great Britain, and the United States
Harold D. Clarke, Marianne C. Stewart, and Gary Zuk, Editors

Executive Leadership in Anglo-American Systems
Colin Campbell, S.J., and Margaret Jane Wyszomirski, Editors

Extraordinary Measures: The Exercise of Prerogative Powers in the United States
Daniel P. Franklin

Foreign Policy Motivation: A General Theory and a Case Study
Richard W. Cottam

Global Competitiveness and Industrial Growth in Taiwan and the Philippines
Cheng-Tian Kuo

"He Shall Not Pass This Way Again": The Legacy of Justice William O. Douglas
Stephen L. Wasby, Editor

History and Context in Comparative Public Policy
Douglas E. Ashford, Editor

Homeward Bound: Explaining Changes in Congressional Behavior
Glenn Parker

How Does Social Science Work? Reflections on Practice
Paul Diesing

Imagery and Ideology in U.S. Policy Toward Libya, 1969–1982
Mahmoud G. ElWarfally

The Impact of Policy Analysis
James M. Rogers

Interests and Institutions: Substance and Structure in American Politics
Robert H. Salisbury

Iran and the United States: A Cold War Case Study
Richard W. Cottam

Japanese Prefectures and Policymaking
Steven R. Reed

The Japanese Prime Minister and Public Policy
Kenji Hayao

Making Common Sense of Japan
Steven R. Reed

Making Regulatory Policy
Keith Hawkins and John M. Thomas, Editors

Managing the Presidency: Carter, Reagan, and the Search for Executive Harmony
Colin Campbell, S.J.

The Moral Dimensions of Public Policy Choice: Beyond the Market Paradigm
John Martin Gillroy and Maurice Wade, Editors

Native Americans and Public Policy
Fremont J. Lyden and Lyman H. Legters, Editors

Organizing Governance, Governing Organizations
Colin Campbell, S.J., and B. Guy Peters, Editors

Party Organizations in American Politics
Cornelius P. Cotter et al.

Perceptions and Behavior in Soviet Foreign Policy
Richard K. Herrmann

Pesticides and Politics: The Life Cycle of a Public Issue
Christopher J. Bosso

Policy Analysis by Design
Davis B. Bobrow and John S. Dryzek

The Political Failure of Employment Policy, 1945–1982
Gary Mucciaroni

Political Leadership: A Source Book
Barbara Kellerman, Editor

Political Leadership in an Age of Constraint: The Australian Experience
Colin Campbell, S.J., and John Halligan

The Political Psychology of the Gulf War: Leaders, Publics, and the Process of Conflict
Stanley A. Renshon, Editor

The Politics of Expert Advice: Creating, Using, and Manipulating Scientific Knowledge for Public Policy
Anthony Barker and B. Guy Peters, Editors

The Politics of the U.S. Cabinet: Representation in the Executive Branch, 1789–1984
Jeffrey E. Cohen

Politics Within the State: Elite Bureaucrats and Industrial Policy in Authoritarian Brazil
Ben Ross Schneider

Post-Passage Politics: Bicameral Resolution in Congress
Stephen D. Van Beek

The Presidency and Public Policy Making
George C. Edwards III, Steven A. Shull, and Norman C. Thomas, Editors

Pressure, Power, and Policy: Policy Networks and State Autonomy in Britain and the United States
Martin J. Smith

Private Markets and Public Intervention: A Primer for Policy Designers
Harvey Averch

The Promise and Paradox of Civil Service Reform
Patricia W. Ingraham and David H. Rosenbloom, Editors

Public Policy in Latin America: A Comparative Survey
John W. Sloan

Reluctant Partners: Implementing Federal Policy
Robert P. Stoker

Researching the Presidency: Vital Questions, New Approaches
George C. Edwards III, John H. Kessel, and Bert A. Rockman, Editors

Roads to Reason: Transportation, Administration, and Rationality in Colombia
Richard E. Hartwig

Scrambling for Protection: The New Media and the First Amendment
Patrick Garry

The SEC and Capital Market Regulation: The Politics of Expertise
Ann M. Khademian

Site Unseen: The Politics of Siting a Nuclear Waste Repository
Gerald Jacob

The Speaker and the Budget: Leadership in the Post-Reform House of Representatives
Daniel J. Palazzolo

The State Roots of National Politics: Congress and the Tax Agenda, 1978–1986
Michael B. Berkman

The Struggle for Social Security, 1900–1935
Roy Lubove

Tage Erlander: Serving the Welfare State, 1946–1969
Olof Ruin

Thatcher, Reagan, Mulroney: In Search of a New Bureaucracy
Donald Savoie

Traffic Safety Reform in the United States and Great Britain
Jerome S. Legge, Jr.